TRANSACTIONS

OF THE

AMERICAN PHILOSOPHICAL SOCIETY

HELD AT PHILADELPHIA
FOR PROMOTING USEFUL KNOWLEDGE

NEW SERIES—VOLUME 63, PART 6
1973

ARMS ACROSS THE BORDER: UNITED STATES AID TO JUÁREZ DURING THE FRENCH INTERVENTION IN MEXICO

ROBERT RYAL MILLER

Professor of History, California State University

THE AMERICAN PHILOSOPHICAL SOCIETY
INDEPENDENCE SQUARE
PHILADELPHIA

December, 1973

Copyright © 1973 by The American Philosophical Society

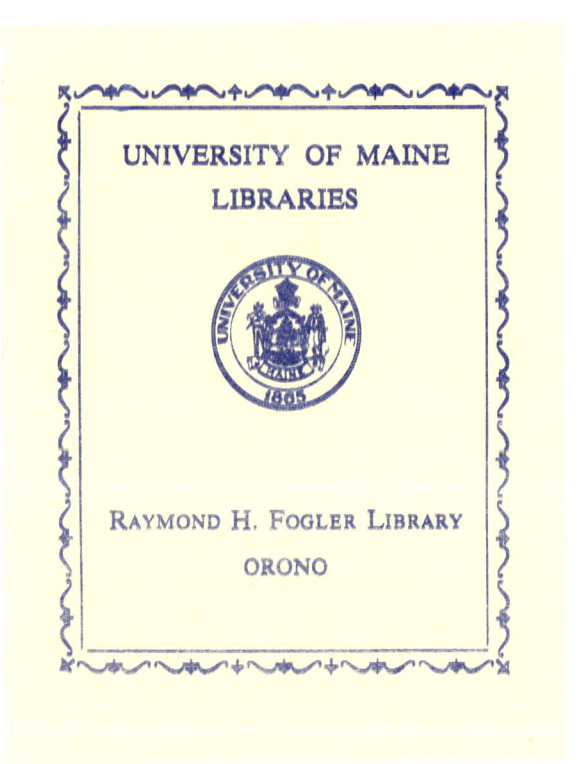

Library of Congress Catalog
Card Number 73-86617
International Standard Book Number 0-87169-636-3

PREFACE

The 1861–1867 French intervention in Mexico spawned a voluminous literature, but some phases of that period have been studied more than others. Most of the accounts center on the establishment and collapse of Mexico's second empire under Maximilian von Hapsburg and his wife Carlotta. The author of a recently published monograph analyzed the French military occupation; others have examined diplomatic relations between various powers, especially the French and Mexican empires. But with the exception of biographies of Benito Juárez, the activities of Mexican republicans during the 1860's have received less attention, and there is no book focusing on military support that the *Juaristas* received from the United States. This study has been written in an attempt to fill that lacuna.

A principal reason for the lack of publications about United States aid to Juárez is that the military supplies were secured by secret agents whose clandestine movements are not easy to trace. At least two dozen Mexican confidential commissioners sought arms in the United States between 1861 and 1867. Some of the men represented state governors; others, military field commanders; and a few were dispatched by President Juárez of the central government. Because the latter were the principal agents, engaged in large-scale operations, their accomplishments and failures form the basis for this study.

Manuscript and published correspondence of the Mexican minister to the United States, supplemented by documents and papers of several Juarist agents, proved to be the best sources for information about this subject. For permission to use their collections and for the splendid research facilities provided, I wish to thank Dr. George P. Hammond, Director Emeritus of the Bancroft Library at the University of California, Berkeley; Miss Caroline Dunn, Librarian of the William Henry Smith Memorial Library of the Indiana Historical Society; and General Ernesto Higuera Pinedo, former Director of the Archivo Histórico Militar of the Secretaría de Defensa Nacional, México, D.F.

Several historians and friends saw preliminary versions of this book and made valuable contributions to it. Professor Abraham Nasatir of California State University, San Diego, kindly pointed out French documents for the topic. Professor Mark Van Aken, my colleague at California State University, Hayward, read parts of the manuscript as did Professors Lawrence Kinnaird and Eric Bellquist of the University of California, Berkeley. I am grateful for their comments and suggestions, and of course exempt them from any errors of fact or interpretation. Finally, I wish to acknowledge the help of my wife, Penny, who typed the manuscript.

R.R.M.

Berkeley, California

ARMS ACROSS THE BORDER:

UNITED STATES AID TO JUÁREZ DURING THE FRENCH INTERVENTION IN MEXICO

Robert Ryal Miller

CONTENTS

	PAGE
I. Background—Mexico in the 1860's	5
II. Matías Romero—Juárez's man in Washington	8
III. General Vega—California arms smuggler	16
IV. Vega's volunteer army	23
V. General Sánchez Ochoa—intrigues with Frémont	30
VI. The American Legion of Honor in Mexico	37
VII. General Wallace—friend of Mexico	41
VIII. General Carvajal—autocrat of the Rio Grande	47
IX. General Sturm—ordnance expediter	53
X. The reckoning—accomplishments and role of the agents	
Bibliography	62
Index	66

I. BACKGROUND—MEXICO IN THE 1860's

The colorful and dramatic figures of Benito Juárez, a Zapotec Indian, and Maximilian von Hapsburg, an Austrian archduke, symbolize opposing sides in the bloody civil war and foreign intervention that wracked Mexico from 1861 to 1867. Culminating decades of struggle between liberals and conservatives, events of that era finally settled the question of whether Mexico should be a republic or a monarchy. In support of the latter principle, and for other reasons, Napoleon III of France sent thousands of Gallic soldiers to Mexico where they conquered much of the country, established a monarchy, and placed Emperor Maximilian on the cactus throne. Meanwhile, by moving his seat of government from place to place in northern Mexico, President Juárez kept the constitutional republic from being extinguished. For several years his generals used Fabian tactics and guerrilla warfare to combat the French and their Mexican imperial allies. But coincident with the French troop withdrawal and with the arrival of modern arms from the United States, the Juaristas mounted a counter-offensive and by July, 1867, triumphantly defeated Maximilian and his empire.

Reasons for the French intervention were related to the chronic condition of political instability and civil war in Mexico. Between 1857 and 1860 the War of the Reform devastated much of the countryside, bankrupted the national treasury, and widened the cleavage between conservatives and liberals. When President Juárez and the liberals won in 1860, the Roman Catholic Church, whose leaders had supported the conservatives, was stripped of many of its prerogatives and forced to give up much of its property. Thus the clergy and their supporters had a deep-seated grievance against the Juárez administration.

Following the defeat of the conservatives in the War of the Reform, Mexican monarchist and clerical leaders continued their political activities from exile in Europe. Miguel Miramón, a former conservative president, had fled to Spain; the bishop of Puebla, Pelagio A. de Labastida y Dávalos, had been banished from Mexico and was in Italy; and General Juan N. Almonte, one of the leading conservative politicians, had his headquarters in Paris. These men, along with a number of other Mexican refugees, tried to interest European sovereigns in aiding their cause and returning them to power.

In addition to the machinations of Mexican monarchists and clericals, another motive behind the intervention was a concerted effort of European monarchs to test and invalidate the Monroe Doctrine. Spain, France, and Great Britain were determined to vindicate their rights in the Western Hemisphere, and they chose to assert their position in the years when the United States was more accurately referred to as the "disunited states." As part of this neo-imperialist scheme, Spain reannexed the Dominican Republic, seized the Chincha Islands off the coast of Peru, and contrived imperial designs for Mexico. According to the United States minister in Madrid in 1861, officials of Queen Isabella's government wanted a Spanish prince or some prince married to a Spanish princess placed on the Mexican throne.[1]

In Paris, Napoleon III had an ambitious foreign policy that embraced the establishment of an empire in Mexico with a monarch selected by him and subservient to commercial and political interests of France. Such a government would check the spirit of American republicanism and at the same time thwart the growing economic and cultural influence of the United States in Latin America. Napoleon's intentions were clearly revealed in his instructions to General Elie Forey, commander of the French expeditionary forces in Mexico in 1862. Part of his letter reads:

---

[1] Carl Schurz to William H. Seward, Madrid, September 27, 1861, U.S. National Archives, Department of State, Diplomatic Dispatches, Spain, Microcopy M-31, Roll 42; see also Schurz, 1911: p. 145.

If a firm government is established there [Mexico] by the aid of France, we shall give to the Latin race beyond the ocean its ancient strength and power ... we shall have extended our benevolent influence to the center of America, and that influence, while it makes a market for our fabrics, secures us the material indispensable to our manufactures.[2]

But the European intervention in Mexico is above all an excellent example of financial imperialism, the utilization of armed forces to collect debts contracted by international bankers. Indeed, the immediate cause as well as the justification for the intervention was provided when the congress of the Republic of Mexico, on July 17, 1861, voted to suspend payment of principal and interest on all foreign debts for two years. President Juárez, recognizing his government's indebtedness to citizens of Spain, France, and England in the amount of $82,315,446, agreed with the moratorium and explained that it was necessary because the treasury was bankrupt.[3] With two years of peace and stability, he expected that payment could be resumed.

As a result of Juárez's action suspending payment of foreign debts, representatives of France, Spain, and Great Britain met in London in the fall of 1861. On the last day of October they signed a treaty, the Convention of London, which called for armed intervention with a force sufficient to seize and occupy fortresses and military positions on the Gulf coast of Mexico. Presumably the sole purpose was to collect debts. The treaty stated that the three powers would not seek any acquisition of territory or any special advantages, nor were they to hinder the right of the Mexican people to choose their form of government and its personnel.[4]

The European intervention in Mexico began in December of 1861 with the arrival of the Spanish contingent at Veracruz, and it continued the following month when French and British troops landed at the same port. Almost immediately the military allies issued a proclamation announcing that they had come only to stretch out a friendly hand to a people suffering from internal disorder; they were going to assist in the "regeneration" of Mexico.[5]

What began as a tripartite invasion was soon transformed into a unilateral one. Jealousy and friction between allied military commanders paralleled disagreements among civilian commissioners accompanying the expedition. The course of action to be followed was unclear and decisions unconcerted. The British ordered a reduction of Mexican import duties by one-half; Spanish officials insisted on a formal diplomatic apology for expelling their ambassador in 1861; and French demands included extraterritoriality, preferential duties, and full recognition of all financial claims.[6] Gradually the British and Spanish representatives realized that they were being tricked into cooperating with an aggressive French policy which went beyond the more limited objectives of debt collection. Finally at a conference of the commissioners held at Orizaba on April 9, 1862, the Spanish and British leaders decided to withdraw their forces from Mexico, leaving the collection of debts to their diplomats. The French remained in Mexico and extended their military operations.

Following a build-up of forces, French troops began to move toward the Mexican capital. When they assaulted the fortified city of Puebla on May 5, 1862, they were humiliatingly defeated and forced to retreat back to the coast. General Ignacio Zaragoza by his brilliant victory gained a year's time for the constitutional government and he added a national holiday to the Mexican calendar, the *cinco de mayo*. But the French sent reinforcements to Mexico, and the following year Puebla surrendered after a two-month siege. The way was now open to the capital. President Juárez and his republican government leaders, forced to evacuate Mexico City, began a series of peregrinations to the north, stopping briefly in San Luis Potosí. From this temporary capital Juárez dispatched the first secret agents to the United States with orders to purchase and forward arms to the republic. Their assignment was difficult because the Civil War in the northern republic led to an embargo on the export of arms.

In Mexico City the French commander began to carry out the schemes of his emperor. He organized a provisional government and, along with the French minister, appointed 285 Mexican conservatives to an Assembly of Notables. This subservient body, with but two days of discussion, declared that Mexico would thereafter be a monarchy with a Catholic prince as emperor. The principal candidate, Maximilian, stated that he could not accept the offer "unless a national manifestation showed in an undoubted manner the desire of the nation to place him on the throne."[7] The plebiscite was easy to arrange in the three Mexican states under French control, and to no one's surprise, the referendum indicated overwhelming approval of the Austrian archduke.

Meanwhile, French forces extended their control in all directions from Mexico City. Campaigns against republican-held cities and fortifications were successful, but bands of Mexican guerrillas constantly threatened the line of communications and made forays on small groups of French troops. To combat this, the French organized a counter-guerrilla unit composed of tough soldiers of fortune from various countries of Europe, the

---

[2] Napoleon III to General Forey, July 5, 1862, in Martin, 1914; pp. 107–108. Differences between original instructions and published version discussed in Hanna and Hanna, 1971: pp. 77–80.

[3] Lefèvre, 1962: p. 295; see also Turlington, 1930: pp. 126-170.

[4] Article IV of the Convention invited the United States to accede to the agreement, but the invitation was refused.

[5] Niox, 1874: 1: pp. 39–40; see also Dabbs, 1963: p. 31.

[6] Musser, 1918: pp. 36–37.

[7] Maximilian to Gutiérrez de Estrada, Miramar, December 8, 1861, in García and Pereyra, 1903: 1: pp. 115–116.

Middle East, and the Americas.[8] Their orders were to clear Mexico of the constitutional irregular forces, an impossible task considering their limited resources and the size of the country.

With the northward advance of the French and their Mexican allies, President Juárez and his mobile cabinet moved from San Luis Potosí to Durango, later fleeing to Saltillo, then Monterrey and Chihuahua. Republican forces held the vast territory of the northern states of Mexico where they believed they could make a final successul stand. The opposing army outnumbered them three to one, but the Juárez government possessed a potent advantage—diplomatic recognition by the United States. President Lincoln's government also refused to treat with representatives of the Mexican empire, and in Secretary of State William Seward's correspondence, Maximilian was referred to as "the so-called emperor of Mexico."

When Emperor Maximilian and his wife Carlotta arrived in their new kingdom during the summer of 1864, monarchist troops by no means held a majority of the country. But the French, with their superior discipline and equipment, continued to push the republican forces toward the northern border. Without a shot being fired, Durango was occupied in July, Saltillo and Monterrey in August, and Matamoros, near the mouth of the Rio Grande, was quietly entered in September of 1864. One writer aptly commented that "the French conquered Mexico with their legs rather than their swords."[9]

The apogee of the French intervention in Mexico was reached in 1865. By April imperial troops under Marshall Bazaine numbered about sixty thousand men, half of whom were French soldiers. During that critical year imperialists secured victories in the states of Oaxaca, Morelia, Sonora, and Chihuahua. In addition, French naval squadrons controlled the waters and ports on Mexico's two coasts. To complete the picture, the monarchist land offensive had confined remnants of the regular republican forces to the Apache Indian country near the Texas and New Mexican border.

These were dark days for Juárez and the republican government of Mexico. They had lost control of every state capital, and the French, by occupying the ports, cut off customhouse receipts and all contact with the outside world except through Texas and New Mexico. Keeping a few steps ahead of the French army, the chief officers of the constitutional government retreated to Paso del Norte, later renamed Ciudad Juárez, on the Mexican-American border. The United States consul in that city reported in December, 1865, that Juárez's forces there numbered only three hundred men.[10] Republican armies had melted away as defeat, defection, and delay in pay took their toll. There was also discord and disgust among the republican government leaders. Several cabinet members and troop commanders broke with Juárez in 1865 when, owing to the wartime inability to hold elections, he extended his term of office unconstitutionally. Hampered by a critical shortage of funds and effective troops, a number of Juarist officers crossed into the United States. There were more than a dozen Mexican generals in New York City in 1865; others were in Texas and California. Many officers requested, and some received, permission to leave Mexico in order to secure financial and material aid for their country.

But in this hour of despair the tide began to turn in favor of the republican cause. In the first place, termination of the Civil War in the United States meant an end to the embargo on arms shipments from that country. It also meant that there was a surplus of military equipment in North American factories and at military bases, and this plethora of weapons coupled with government surplus disposal policy forced the price of munitions down radically. The end of the war also brought about wholesale discharge of soldiers, many of whom went to Mexico as mercenaries. A few Union veterans and a considerable number of Confederates joined Maximilian's imperial forces, while a still greater number of northern veterans joined units of the Mexican republican army.[11]

Another important determinant in Juárez's favor was the French decision to abandon their Mexican crusade. At the end of 1865 Napoleon III announced that French troops would be withdrawn from Mexico in three detachments. The first group was to depart in November, 1866, the second to leave four months later, and the final embarkation was scheduled for November of 1867. The French expeditionary commander was instructed to make a vigorous attempt to crush Juárez's forces before leaving, and as part of this final effort, the famous "Black Flag Decree" of October, 1865, was issued. This order, signed by Maximilian, stipulated that all who were caught fighting the imperialists were to be summarily executed without trial. As might have been expected, this decree only increased the cleavage between the two governments and inflamed the fury of Mexico's fratricidal strife.

Before sailing home, the French commander helped Maximilian form new armies composed of Mexicans loyal to the empire along with Austrian and Belgian volunteers, but the withdrawal of French soldiers

---

[8] Keratry, 1868: pp. 9-10; Dabbs, 1963: p. 35.
[9] Loizillon, 1890: p. 152.
[10] Henry Cuniffe to William H. Seward, Paso del Norte, Mexico, December 29, 1865, U.S. National Archives, Department of State, Consular Dispatches, Ciudad Juárez, Microcopy M-184, Roll 1; see also dispatches dated January 12, July 12, 1866.
[11] See chapter VI for details on foreign volunteers in Mexico.

spelled the collapse of the Mexican empire. As the French retreated from the north, republican forces occupied the abandoned cities and forts. Juárez was back in Chihuahua by March, 1866, and the same month Matamoros capitulated to the republicans. One by one the cities were liberated; a chronological listing of them resembles a schedule of railroad stops. Meanwhile, much farther south, General Porfirio Díaz escaped from his French captors and quickly assembled a loyal army that recaptured Oaxaca. About the same time, the republicans regained control of the state of Guerrero.

In February of 1867 Marshall Bazaine at the head of the remaining French troops left Mexico City for the port of Veracruz. Before leaving Mexico he urged Maximilian to abdicate, but the emperor decided to cast his lot with his Mexican followers. In fact, he took to the field at the head of his troops, determined to make a stand at Querétaro. The dramatic events that accompanied the siege of that city were climaxed by the capture, trial, and execution of Maximilian. By July of 1867 Mexico's empire had collapsed and Juárez was back in the presidential chair in Mexico City.

The fortunes of the republican government during the French intervention rose and fell in inverse proportion to the success and failure of the monarchists. When Juarist forces began to receive modern military hardware and volunteers from the United States, and when the French troops began to retreat, the former were able to mount an offensive and win battles. Yankee volunteers, experienced in the handling of repeating rifles and artillery, were enlisted by secret agents who held commissions from President Juárez. These commissioners were also responsible for forwarding rifles, torpedoes, artillery pieces, ammunition, uniforms, medical equipment, and other military supplies that converted the republican forces from ragged guerrilla bands with obsolete weapons, even bows and arrows, to a well-equipped and triumphant phalanx. Directing the activities of these Mexican agents was Juárez's diplomatic representative in Washington, Don Matías Romero, who served there during most of the French intervention. Romero's accomplishments and failures during those years will be summarized in the following chapter.

II. MATÍAS ROMERO—JUÁREZ'S MAN IN WASHINGTON

The central figure in the story of United States aid to Juárez during the French intervention was Mexico's diplomatic representative in Washington, Matías Romero. His task was not an easy one since both Mexico and the United States were torn by civil wars which interrupted communications and presented grave problems in international relations. But this brilliant young man was able to carry out his diplomatic duties while thwarting agents of Napoleon III, Maximilian, and the Confederacy. He was also a key figure in the purchase of several million dollars worth of munitions, in directing propaganda favorable to the Mexican republic, and in attempts to float a fifty million dollar loan. At the same time he coordinated the activities of a dozen and a half Juarist secret agents operating in the United States.

Before considering in detail the tasks and accomplishments of Matías Romero a few biographical notes may be of interest, especially since there is no published biography of this diplomat-statesman. Such obscurity is undeserved for a man who was once postmaster-general of Mexico, three times minister of the treasury, senator and deputy in the Mexican legislature, a promoter and official of Mexican railroads, editor of thousands of pages of documents, author of several books and more than twenty published articles in English and Spanish, an organizer of the Pan American Union, and envoy to the United States intermittently over a period of forty years.[1]

Romero's political career was enhanced if not determined entirely by having been born in Oaxaca, the birthplace of Benito Juárez, Porfirio Díaz, Ignacio Mariscal, and other national leaders of his time. Born in 1837, he was a precocious child and prodigious student, winning prizes and other distinctions at Oaxaca's Institute of Arts and Sciences. In 1855 at the age of eighteen he went to Mexico City to continue studies in law aided by a former director of the Oaxaca Institute, Benito Juárez, who was then serving as minister of justice in the national cabinet. With Juárez's influence Romero obtained a modest, part-time position in the ministry of foreign relations where he made a thorough study of the archives of that department, publishing in 1859 a guide to Mexico's treaties with foreign nations. Although he received his lawyer's title in 1857, Romero was not permitted to practice law because he was under the minimum age of twenty-one. During the civil war known as *La Reforma*, 1857–1860, he worked closely with the liberal party serving in the army and later as private secretary to Melchor Ocampo, *ministro universal* in Juárez's cabinet. Romero was a member of the small group that accompanied President Juárez and the fugitive cabinet to Colima, then Veracruz, via Panama and New Orleans in 1859.

In December of 1859 Matías Romero was named first secretary of the Mexican legation in Washington; eight months later he became chief of the Mexican delega-

---

[1] A preliminary version of this chapter was published in the *Hispanic American Historical Review* **45**: pp 228–245; permission to reprint it granted by Duke University Press. A biography of Romero by Harry Bernstein has been announced for 1973 publication by the Fondo de Cultura Económica in Mexico. Biographical data on Romero in Peral, 1944: p. 712; Godoy, 1898: p. 222. Partial list of Romero's publications in fol. 242, Archivo Histórico de Matías Romero, Banco de Mexico, México, D.F., and microfilm copy, Bancroft Library, cited hereafter as AHMR.

tion in the United States, holding that position under different titles from chargé d'affaires to ambassador for some twenty-four non-consecutive years. Ambassador Romero died in New York City on December 30, 1898. With the exception of five months in 1863 when he briefly served as a colonel in the Mexican army, Matías Romero represented the Mexican republic in Washington during the entire period of the French intervention, 1861–1867.[2]

Romero's interest in inter-American affairs extended to the personal level where he counted among his friends a number of influential persons in Washington. Perhaps he was closest to General Ulysses S. Grant, an intimacy "the more remarkable because Grant, as a rule, was not fond of foreigners. . . ."[3] When he had the funds, Romero hosted dinner parties and other social events in the Mexican embassy. Accepting one invitation the president's son, Robert Lincoln, remarked, "I hope I may be able to come off unscathed by your double attractions—the ladies and the table."[4] Speaking of ladies, Romero apparently was friendly with more than one Yankee belle. In March, 1867, when it was rumored by General and Mrs. Grant that Romero was engaged to be married to an American widow who had a nineteen-year-old daughter, a mutual friend advised him to marry the girl rather than her mother. The following year Romero married a young American girl, Lucretia (Lula) Allen, with whom he had a happy marriage lasting until her death thirty years later.[5]

Many times during his residence in Washington Matías Romero visited the White House to confer with the president. But one unique presidential visit took place on January 19, 1861, when he went to Springfield, Illinois, to confer with Abraham Lincoln in the interim between the latter's election and inauguration. Romero, who was only twenty-three years old at the time, gave an account of the interview in his diary, an excerpt of which follows:

> He told me that during his administration he would endeavor to do anything within his power in favor of the interests of Mexico. Then I told him that Mexico rejoiced with the triumph of the Republican party because she hoped that the policy of this party would be more loyal and friendly and not like that of the Democrats who had stooped to take territory from Mexico in order to extend slavery.[6]

FIG. 1. Don Matías Romero, Mexican minister to the United States. Photo courtesty of Seward House, Auburn, New York.

Don Matías certainly had the talent for a diplomatic or political career!

William H. Seward, Lincoln's secretary of state, was the American to whom Romero addressed the majority of his diplomatic correspondence in the 1860's. Of course relations with Mexico were not Seward's principal concern—the overshadowing problem was the Civil War and the possibility that some European nation might recognize and assist the Confederate States of America. But on this very point the intervention in Mexico and the rebellion in the United States were interrelated, for French troops invaded Mexico at the same time that France appeared a potential ally of the Confederacy. Indeed, the Confederate agent John Slidell twice in 1862 offered Napoleon III support for his Mexican venture in return for recognition or intervention in the Civil War, but both times was refused. Southern agents were also unsuccessful with Maximilian who rebuffed their attempts to gain recognition,

---

[2] For data on Romero's education, see Mexico, Legación, Circulares, 1868: 2: pp. 393–400; Ramírez, 1948: pp. 78–83. Obituaries in New York Times, December 31, 1898, p. 6; Mexico, Secretaría de Relaciones Exteriores, 1899: pp. 169–171.

[3] Badeau, 1888: p. 391. Romero-Grant friendship and business relationship in AHMR, fol. 2014, 2058, 50062, 50073; see also Pletcher, 1958: pp. 13–14, 152–153, 157–164.

[4] Robert Lincoln to Romero, February 18, 1864, AHMR, fol. 290.

[5] James Beekman to Romero, March 21, 1867, AHMR, fol. 1649; marriage details in fol. 2547, 2565, 2582, 2610. Lucretia Allen Romero's obituary in Washington Star, July 30, 1898, p. 7.

[6] Romero, 1960: p. 378; see also Hildner, 1950: pp. 184–189.

nor did Mexican imperial agents in Washington ever get so much as an interview with the American president or secretary of state. Later when the French offered to withdraw from Mexico provided the United States would recognize Maximilian's empire, Seward refused to be a party to that bargain.[7]

Romero continually maintained that the intervention and rebellion were but two phases of the same movement. Speaking of the French aggression in Mexico, he once told Seward that "one of the objects of the expedition was to acquire a base of operations against the United States," and he added that when Napoleon III enlarged his new dependency he would "greatly rely upon the French element which predominates in the population of Louisiana, and upon the blindness of the leaders of the southern insurrection. . . ."[8]

The same theme is echoed in one of the books about Mexico published in the 1860's: "Napoleon has established a monarchy in Mexico, to which he will annex Texas, and to this will be annexed, in time, all the southern states."[9]

Romero's attitude about the interrelationship between the rebellion and intervention was a reflection of a considerable body of public opinion in the United States. Many of those who held that point of view went on to say that the northern republic should uphold the Monroe Doctrine and help Mexico evict the French, but most agreed that any assistance would have to wait the defeat of the Confederacy. In the early part of 1862 Montgomery Blair, postmaster-general in Lincoln's cabinet, told the Mexican minister that the French would be driven from Mexico when the Civil War ended. Shortly thereafter President Lincoln assured Romero that settlement of the Mexican question was dependent upon events in the United States.[10] Four potential presidential candidates in 1864, Lincoln, Grant, Frémont, and McClellan, publicly stated their determination to sustain the Monroe Doctrine and to oppose the political intervention of France in the New World.[11] Two of Romero's friends in Congress were more outspoken; they introduced resolutions protesting the European invasion. Senator James McDougall's resolution demanding the withdrawal of the French troops was tabled, but that of Representative Henry Winter Davis passed unanimously on April 4, 1864. The declaration called attention to the "deplorable events" in Mexico and stated that "it does not accord with the policy of the United States to acknowledge a monarchical government, erected on the ruins of any republican government in America, under the auspices of any European power." It should be noted that Romero previously had called upon Davis urging such action.[12]

The role of Romero as a propaganda agent should not be overlooked, for, while there was much sentiment in the United States favorable to the Mexican republic, some of it was deliberately fomented by the Mexican representative. In addition to publishing and distributing thousands of copies of a biography of President Juárez and hundreds of pamphlets calling attention to the plight of Mexico, Romero furnished a constant stream of news and informative articles to selected newspaper in the United States. For the Mexican foreign office he compiled a list of twenty-five American newspapers which he thought should receive materials from the Mexican government to help shape favorable public opinion. Editors of the New York *Times,* Romero felt, had the most complete understanding of affairs in Mexico, but many of the articles he sent them and to the New York *Herald* were not published because he "lacked the means to compensate the publishers."[13]

The Mexican minister also participated in and sponsored a series of public banquets in order to get publicity for his country. At the same time he was complying with his instructions which obliged him "to get from the people of this country [United States] public demonstrations in favor of our [Mexican] cause."[14] Several of the propaganda dinners were held at Delmonico's, one of New York's finest restaurants, where during and after eight-course dinners Romero's guests heard a number of toasts and speeches about Mexico and inter-American friendship. The orchestral accompaniment carried out the international theme; at one banquet they played "selections from operas, some Mexican tunes, alternating with 'Yankee Doodle' and 'Hail Columbia.'"[15]

Invitations to Romero's dinners bore the names of distinguished Americans who served as co-sponsors. William Cullen Bryant, poet and editor of the New York *Evening Post,* attended several of the banquets along with James W. Beekman, a wealthy landowner; David Hoadley, president of the Panama Railroad Company; John W. Hammersley, a noted New York lawyer; and William H. Aspinwall, promoter of the Panama Railroad, owner of the Pacific Mail Steamship Line, and one of the richest men in New York. Historian and diplomat George Bancroft addressed the banquet held on March 29, 1864; in addition to his remarks and those of Romero, the guests listened to

---

[7] Owsley, 1959: p. 507; Rippy, 1926: pp. 243–244; Frazer, "Maximilian's Propaganda," 1944: p. 6; U.S. Congress, *House Exec. Doc.* 20: pp. 9–10.

[8] Mexico, Legación, 1870–1892: 2: p. 745.

[9] Flint, 1867: pp. 8–9.

[10] Mexico, Legación, 1870–1892: 2: pp. 170–171, 184.

[11] Iglesias, 1868: 2: pp. 313–314; see also Mexico, Legación, 1870–1892: 2: p. 257.

[12] U.S. Congress, *Congressional Globe,* April 4, 1864, p. 1408; see also Mexico, Legación, 1870–1892: 4: pp. 9, 17, 20–21.

[13] Mexico, Legación, 1870–1892: 3: p. 491; the 27-p. biography of Juárez is listed with Romero's writings, AHMR, fol. 242.

[14] Mexico, Legación, *Circulares,* 1868: 2: p. 37.

[15] *Ibid.,* pp. 5–180, 316–392; another banquet mentioned in AHMR, fol. 242; see also Mexico, Legación, 1870–1892: 3: pp. 570–573, 606–613.

short speeches by nineteen men including the president of Columbia University and the mayor of New York City.[16]

Romero's banquet speeches accurately reflect his opinions as indicated in his diary and correspondence for those years. In one address he traced the history of Mexican-American relations, blaming the slaveholding class for all the past antagonisms between the two countries. Then noting that there were many commercial opportunities in Mexico, he indicated that his government would grant liberal economic concessions to Americans. "When that was done," he said, "the United States would gain all the advantages that could be obtained from annexing Mexico without acquiring any of the inconveniences that such a step would produce."[17] As for the French intervention, Romero said he knew that the United States would eventually come to Mexico's aid, but in the meantime he thought that the northern power should make it clear to Europe that it opposed the aggression.

The European invasion of Mexico and the concurrent attempts of Spain to regain her New World colonies prompted leaders of other American republics to propose joint action and treaties of common defense. Strongly endorsed by Romero, diplomats of Peru and Chile endeavored unsuccessfully to get the United States to join in a league of mutual guarantees. One of the proposals called for a Pan American Congress to meet in Washington, D. C.; another envisaged a diplomatic treaty which would guarantee the independence, integrity, and autonomy of the New World nations. But Seward indicated that the Civil War and strained relations with Europe precluded United States participation in such a movement, while Romero, working through Senator Charles Sumner, could not move the American secretary of state from that stand. Meanwhile, in a note to Romero, General Tomás de Mosquera of Colombia offered to raise an army of 15,000 men and march across Central America to aid Mexico in her "Second War of Independence." He noted the similarity of such an expedition to the famous campaigns of his compatriot, Simón Bolívar. Although Latin American leaders talked of "grand armies" to aid Mexico, issued declarations and resolutions against the French, and named President Juárez "Benemérito [hero] of the Americas," their assistance was of little consequence to the struggling republic.[18]

What did help the Juaristas in their war against the French was the steady flow of arms and munitions forwarded from the United States by agents under the direction of Minister Romero. Mexico had no manufacturers of arms, so these essentials had to be secured outside the country. Since the French navy controlled both coasts of Mexico during the intervention, and there was no possibility of obtaining arms overland from Central America, the United States was the logical and primary source for war material. But the Civil War in the "dis-United States" created an unusual domestic demand for military hardware, and in addition the Union government prohibited the export of munitions, seeking to keep them out of the Confederacy. Thus the arms that were sent to Mexico during the Civil War had to be smuggled across the border. To be sure, some fantastic ruses were attempted such as exporting the arms via Canada, transferring them at a high-seas rendezvous, and concealing them in barrels of pickles.

In Washington, Romero worked continually to have the prohibition on the export of arms revoked. He had many personal interviews with the secretary of war and other members of Lincoln's cabinet, pointing out to them the absolute necessity of such action to save his republic. But the ban was not lifted until the spring of 1865 after the end of the Civil War. Even then United States officials continued to obstruct arms shipments to Mexico; in one case Romero had to appeal to Secretary Seward, General Grant, and Attorney-General Speed before an export ban by a United States general was rescinded.[19] Earlier Romero had written to Seward saying:

The fact that...[the United States] Government has prohibited, to our hurt, the exporting of arms from the United States...has had the result that from the beginning of the war the Government of Mexico has met with such a reduced quantity of rifles, and those in such poor condition, that it is truly remarkable how it has been possible to prolong the resistence [sic] with such ramshackle materials.[20]

Meanwhile, operating clandestinely from 1862 to 1865 then openly for the next two years, a series of special Mexican agents negotiated arms purchases in the United States for shipment to the Juárez forces. Romero himself headed the list of secret commissioners, for in addition to his authority as head of the Mexican legation he had certain confidential powers and functions. For example, he was authorized to raise a volunteer force of several thousand Americans and to commission as many as five men as generals in the Mexican army. He also had twenty letters of marque from his government, which he was perpared to issue.[21] But most important, Romero served as coordinator of the dozen and a half Juarist secret agents in the United States in the 1860's. His job was difficult owing to the

---

[16] Mexico, Legación, *Circulares*, 1868: 2: pp. 57–132.
[17] *Ibid.*, p. 92; see also pp. 87–98.
[18] Message from executive of Argentina, May 25, 1862, AHMR, fol. 188; Peruvian consul in New York to Romero, June 17, 1864, AHMR, fol. 398; President of El Salvador to Romero, May 30, 1865, AHMR, fol. 667; notation of Gen. Mosquera's offer, February 28, 1865, AHMR, fol. 587; decree of Colombian Congress, May 2, 1865, AHMR, fol. 646. See also Mexico, Legación, 1870–1892: 2: pp. 26–27, 52, 137–138; Frazer, 1948: pp. 377–388.

[19] U.S. Congress, *House Exec. Doc. 73*: 2: pp. 229–230.
[20] Mexico, Legación, 1870–1892: 5: pp. 506–509.
[21] Romero's special powers in *ibid.* 6: pp. 121–124, 506–507; 9: 449-450. See also Iglesias Calderón, 1907: pp. 24–27.

slow communications of that period and because the men whose work he was coordinating refused to cooperate with each other or to inform him of their plans, accomplishments, and frustrations. Several of the commissioners judged their power to be equal to and independent of the Mexican minister; nevertheless he managed to oversee their major undertakings, report their successes and failures to the Mexican government, and to rescue them from time to time when they became involved in legal and financial troubles.

Besides Romero and his colleagues in the diplomatic and consular service, the Juárez government sent three special commissioners to the United States in the 1860's: Generals Plácido Vega, Gaspar Sánchez Ochoa, and José María Carvajal. The activities of those men will be examined in subsequent chapters. At least fifteen subordinate Mexican agents also appeared in San Francisco, New Orleans, New York, and Washington, sent there by Mexican governors and local military commanders.[22] The primary assignment of all these emissaries was to secure financial and military assistance for their beleaguered republic, and they forwarded to Mexico tons of ammunition, hundreds of thousands of guns, medical and other military stores. Two of the agents, Generals Sánchez Ochoa and Carvajal, floated Mexican bonds in the amount of $40,000,000 in the San Francisco and New York markets. They also organized pro-Mexican clubs in various American communities, established and supported Spanish-language newspapers, and in other ways used secret service funds for propaganda purposes. Through their recruiting efforts, several thousand Americans crossed the Rio Grande and served in the Juarist armies. But the Mexican minister was obliged to terminate the missions of Vega, Sánchez Ochoa, and Carvajal and order those generals to return to Mexico because they exceeded their authority by signing all sorts of contracts making fantastic promises to speculative adventurers such as John C. Frémont.[23]

Directly related to arms purchases was the problem of paying for them. Financial considerations plagued Romero and his government in those years; in fact foreign intervention was brought on by a series of financial crises in Mexico. In the subsequent struggle Juárez tried to maintain armies while actually controlling very little territory, profitable customhouses, or other revenue-producing sources; consequently the republic depended heavily on domestic and foreign loans. Although Romero was involved with several attempts to negotiate loans in the United States, for the most part these efforts were unsuccessful. In 1861 Thomas Corwin, United States minister to Mexico, negotiated a treaty whereby the United States would assume the payment of interest on Mexico's funded debts for five years, the money to be repayed at six per cent interest and "secured by a specific lien upon all the public lands and mineral rights in . . . Lower California, Chihuahua, Sonora, and Sinaloa."[24] But the United States Senate never approved this Mexican loan treaty. In 1866 a proposal to have the United States government guarantee a thirty-million-dollar bond issue of the Mexican republic was also vetoed in Washington. As will be seen in chapter IX, the Mexican bonds were eventually traded to North American munitions firms for military goods, augmenting the firepower if not the revenue of Juárez's forces.

Juarist diplomatic agents were so pressed for funds during the French intervention that they served for months at a time without any salary. The obstinate Romero even resigned his post in 1862 hoping thereby to gain his back pay. But his government replied that critical circumstances precluded the payment and demanded his presence in Washington. A few years later Romero was asked to give a reception and dinner for President Juárez's wife who was living in exile in New York City, but he had to decline because he lacked the means to pay for the affair. About the same time the Mexican consul in New York, Juan N. Navarro, asked Romero, "Is there still no hope of money? My family is literally dying of hunger."[25]

A few nations such as Guatemala, Colombia, Chile, and Holland contributed money to Romero's government;[26] limited credit was extended by private bankers; and some funds were advanced by entrepreneurs who requested business concessions. Regarding the latter, Juárez advised his minister to Washington:

Persons will not be lacking who...will counsel you, as a measure of high politics, to accept any offer, even when it might involve a great sacrifice of the national honor.... Hear with distrust and repulse with energy their suggestions, working as you believe most fitting for the dignity and wellbeing of our nation.[27]

Even the American secretary of state cautioned Romero about the price of foreign aid, telling him that for every million dollars from the United States, Mexico would lose a state, and for every firearm an acre of mineral land.[28] Romero's correspondence for the 1860's contains a number of petitions for grants and concessions. One letter requested an extension of time to commence

---

[22] Lesser agents included: Dr. Juan A. Zambrano, Gov. Juan José Baz, Gen. Pedro de Baranda, Gen. Jesús Díaz de León, Cmdr. Justiniano de Zubiría, Col. Juan Bustamante, Col. Enrique A. Mejía, Col. Bernardino Smith, Lt. Col. Henry R. B. MacIvar, Capt. A. Beasley, Manuel Armendáriz, Felipe de Arellano, Francisco N. Borden, José Ferrer, Juan Romero (brother of Matías Romero), and Andrés Treviño.

[23] See chapter V for Frémont's connection.

[24] U.S. Congress, *House Exec. Doc. 100*, p. 22; Van Deusen, 1967: p. 366.

[25] Navarro to Romero, April 2, 1866, AHMR, fol. 951; Gen. Blas Brúznal to Romero, February 26, 1866, AHMR, fol. 903; J. M. Macías to Romero, March 13, 1867, AHMR, fol. 1624; Romero, 1960: xv.

[26] Bancroft, 1888: **6**: p. 207 and note.

[27] Quoted by García, 1904: pp. 136–137.

[28] *Ibid.*, p. 143.

drilling for petroleum, another asked for a contract to lay a telegraph cable between Cuba and Mexico, a third petitioner wanted to introduce "camels in the desert of Chihuahua and the Asiatic buffalo on the banks of the Rio Grande," and the Mexican-American Railroad Company sought a renewal of grants that had been canceled because of the war. All were willing to pay in advance for concessions and monopolies.[29]

Authorized by his government, Romero granted concessions to several American companies. One of these, the Mexican Mineral and Colonization Company headed by Jacob Leese of Monterey, California, by its 1864 contract approved by President Juárez, promised to pay $100,000 in gold for the unoccupied government-owned land in Baja, California, between 24°20′ and 30° north latitude. Leese, backed by some New York bankers, planned to exploit the mineral deposits of that area and to settle at least two hundred families there within five years. Although the colonization scheme was unsuccessful, Leese did advance money for his contract, and Romero used the funds to buy arms for Mexico.[30] A similar case was that of the Mexican Company of the Pacific whose president was Edward Lee Plumb, American diplomat and friend of Romero. It is interesting to note that in 1864 Romero received 500 shares worth $100 per share of this Pennsylvania-chartered company.[31]

Mexican clubs in the United States were another source of revenue for the Mexican republic in the 1860's. The Society of Friends of Mexico, with headquarters in Baltimore, sent letters throughout the country seeking monetary subscriptions to aid Juárez. The Defenders of the Monroe Doctrine were active in the New Orleans area, while the Monroe Doctrine Committee held public meetings in New York, and the Monroe League did likewise in San Francisco. Other groups included the Mexican Aid Society with branches in Cincinnati and other Midwest cities, Sons of Colombia, Mexican Patriot Club, and affiliated Mexican clubs claiming members in a dozen cities from New York to California. The head of the Mexican Donation Society forwarded some money to Romero saying, "I want it, little as the amount is, to be doing Mexico some good."[32] These organizations assisted Romero's government by publicizing the plight of Mexico, through their contributions of money, and by encouraging volunteers for military service in Mexico.

The whole question of recruiting men in the United States for service in Mexico was complicated by neutrality laws of the United States and by the Civil War and its aftermath. Some three thousand Americans, mostly Union veterans, did join the army of Mexicans who were trying to overthrow the French-imposed empire, but it should be added that about two thousand others, many of them ex-Confederate soldiers, fought with Maximilian's troops.[33]

An attractive army pay scale and a liberal land bonus for veterans enticed many Yankees to fight for the Mexican republic in the post-Civil War period. The monthly pay, comparable to that paid in the United States Army, ranged from $15 for privates to $45 for lieutenants, $205 for colonels, and $500 for major generals. The bonus amounted to land valued at $1,000 for all non-commissioned officers, $1,500 for lieutenants and captains, $2,000 for field-grade officers. Veterans could choose the location of their property from government land in any Mexican state, and the property with improvements was to be exempt from taxes for five years. Foreign military volunteers were also granted full Mexican citizenship. Pamphlets outlining these provisions were printed in California and New York and distributed throughout the United States.[34]

Romero's correspondence is full of letters from Americans and Europeans who wanted to enlist in the Juarist armies, but while volunteers were encouraged, the men were advised to go to Mexico on their own where they would be incorporated into the republican army. One applicant, a Captain Jewett, had served in the Russian army in the Crimean War, then in the Union forces during the Civil War, while another commission seeker had been forced to leave Germany because of his "republican sympathies." One of the most persistent was Erik Wulff who volunteered for special duty saying, "The more desperate an undertaking you put me to carry out, the more I like it, provided you leave the details to me."[35] Some regional recruiting centers were established by Mexican secret agents; they operated openly, even advertising in the metropolitan newspapers. But Romero, although exhorted by the New York *Tribune* to issue a general call for volunteers, decided such a move would be unwise,

---

[29] AHMR, fol. 1002, 1178, 1356, 2105, 2113, 2119, 2124, 2129.

[30] Mexico, Legación, 1870–1892: **7**: pp. 477–479; Ministro de Relaciones Exteriores to Romero, January 18, 1866, AHMR, fol. 841; Mexico, Secretaría de Relaciones Exteriores, 1923–1938: **12**.

[31] Shares transferred April 22, 1864, AHMR, fol. 370; Mexico, Legación, 1870–1892: **4**: p. 131.

[32] AHMR, fol. 398, 1783; Iglesias, 1868: **1**: p. 353; Dabbs, 1963: p. 151; Harrington, 1948: pp. 132–133, 193; Gen. Lew Wallace to Thomas Buchanan Reed, April 30, 1865, Lew Wallace Collection, Indiana Historical Society; U.S. Congress, *House Exec. Doc. 73:* **1**: p. 611; Mexican Club reports in Plácido Vega Papers, **1**: fol. 615–695, Bancroft Library.

[33] Ex-Confederate volunteer strength in O'Connor, 1953: p. 280; see also Sheridan's exaggerated estimate of 10,000 in Sheridan to Grant, June 26, 1865, U.S. Congress *House Exec. Doc. 73:* **2**: p. 463. Romero's report on Yankees fighting for Juárez in Mexico, Legación, 1870–1892: **9**: pp. 412–413.

[34] Law of August 11, 1864, in *Decrees of the Mexican Constitutional Republican Government . . .*, 1864; compare U.S. Army pay in 1865, Hamersly, 1881: pt. 2: p. 192.

[35] Volunteers: AHMR, fol. 356, 358, 366, 642, 654, 729, 753, 998, 1242, 1545, 1546, 1574, 2060.

especially since it would be contrary to his instructions.[36]

In addition to individuals and small groups crossing the Rio Grande to bear arms for the Juárez government, Romero reported plans for large-scale military movements destined to aid his government. Some of the schemes seem fantastic when viewed by a later perspective of history. Such was a proposal in the fall of 1864 in the Confederate senate that an offensive and defensive alliance be celebrated between the Union and Confederacy to vindicate the Monroe Doctrine; the combined armies of the re-United States would then eject the French from Mexico and overthrow the British domination of Canada.[37]

About the same time, Francis P. Blair, an old political journalist who had considerable influence in the Lincoln administration, suggested that peace between North and South might be made on the basis of a joint expedition to expel Maximilian and the French from Mexico. Armed with a permit from Lincoln, Blair crossed through the lines, met with Jefferson Davis in Richmond early in 1865, and arranged the unsuccessful Hampton Roads Conference of February 3, 1865. At that meeting, Secretary Seward insisted on union first, while the Confederates proposed an armistice during which the French could be driven from Mexico.[38]

Romero saw the danger of such foreign military intervention in his country, and realizing that the plan might lead to war between France and the United States, predicted that it would not be accepted. He later suggested to Juárez that "it is better if we do not use a foreign force to save Mexico."[39] The threat to Mexico was that French invaders would be replaced by Yankees. Indeed, Francis Blair told Jefferson Davis that:

He who expels the Bonaparte-Hapsburg dynasty from our Southern flank ... will ally his name with those of Washington and Jackson as a defender of the liberty of the country. If in delivering Mexico he should model its States in form and principle to adapt them to our Union and add a new Southern constellation to its benignant sky while rounding off our possession on the continent at the Isthmus ... he would complete the work of Jefferson. ...[40]

Before the fate of the Blair plan was known, General Lew Wallace offered a similar solution to terminate the wars in the United States and Mexico. He proposed a truce during which Yankees and Rebels would combine to launch an assault on the French in Mexico. With General Grant's permission and with Romero's cooperation, Wallace went to Texas in March of 1865 where he met with a Confederate general and later a Mexican governor. But as will be explained in chapter VII, Wallace's plan was not accepted by higher Confederate officials.

Meanwhile, Montgomery Blair, son of Francis P. Blair and postmaster-general in Lincoln's cabinet from 1861 to 1863, elaborated on and explained his father's plan to Matías Romero. He proposed a joint expedition of 20,000 Union and Confederate soldiers to be commanded by Jefferson Davis, with his division commanders being William T. Sherman and Robert E. Lee. Blair also suggested a premium of $100,000 for the commander, and $30,000 for each of his two subordinate generals. Romero forwarded these ideas to the Mexican foreign minister and, to his surprise, received authorization to execute the plan. The Mexican government had two reservations: that the plan be carried out with the full approval of the United States government, and that a guarantee be secured that the army would not violate the independence of Mexico nor annex any of her territory. The foreign minister also suggested that the number of ex-Confederate soldiers be limited to one-third of the total force.[41]

Romero's authorization to organize an American expeditionary force arrived in Washington about the same time that General Lee surrendered and Abraham Lincoln was assassinated. The unforeseen change in government prompted Romero to seek an interview with the new president, and a confidential meeting between the two was solicited through ex-Senator Preston King, an intimate friend of President Andrew Johnson. King notified Romero, "the President will see you on Monday 24th. ... Thanks for the excellent cigars."[42] During the private interview Romero outlined the history of the French intervention, the problems of Juárez's government, and he emphasized the identity of interests of the two neighboring republics.[43]

The end of the Civil War brought General Grant back to Washington where Romero tried to persuade him to accept command of the proposed army of veterans who would emigrate to Mexico as soldier-colonists. The Mexican diplomat even compared the expeditionary force to that of Lafayette in the American Revolution. Flattered by the remarks and confidence shown by Romero, the general promised his wholehearted support of the project but declined the leadership saying that he could be more useful to Mexico in Washington. Grant and Romero had a private interview on May 8, 1865; the following evening the general and six members of his staff dined at the Mexican legation; four days later Romero accompanied Grant to the general's

---

[36] Mexico, Legación, 1870–1892: **7**: pp. 819–820; see advertisements in New York *Herald,* May 6, 7, 12, 1865; Washington *Chronicle,* May 5, 1865.

[37] Mexico, Legación, 1870–1892: **4**: pp. 407–408.

[38] Johnson and Malone, 1928–1936: **2**: p. 332.

[39] Romero to Juárez [draft], August 24, 1865, AHMR, fol. 724; Mexico, Legación, 1870–1892: **5**: pp. 44–45.

[40] Quoted in Nicolay and Hay, 1890: **10**: pp. 101–102.

[41] Mexico, Legación, 1870–1892: **5**: pp. 4–5, 44–45; **6**: pp. 121–125.

[42] King to Romero, April 20, 1865, AHMR, fol. 643.

[43] Mexico, Legación, 1870–1892: **5**: pp. 259–261.

home in Philadelphia where he was Grant's house guest for four days.⁴⁴

In mid May of 1865, with Grant's advice and assistance, Romero sought a military leader for the proposed expedition. He first interviewed General William Tecumseh Sherman who expressed interest in the plight of Mexico, but who was determined to retire to private life. General Philip Sheridan was another possibility, but he was valuable in his strategic position as commander of the Division of the Gulf with about 100,000 soldiers along the Rio Grande frontier. Sheridan, whose views toward Mexico were almost identical with Grant's, aided the Mexican republicans by demonstrating along the border and by making surplus arms available to them.⁴⁵ Romero's final choice as military commander was General John McAllister Schofield, then in North Carolina, but who said that he would soon be in Washington where he could talk further with Romero, Grant, and President Johnson.

A few weeks later Romero and Schofield signed a little-known contract which outlined the organization and plans for the auxiliary army. Romero previously had received authorization from his government to make such an agreement. The nine major points of the Romero-Schofield agreement were: Schofield agreed to accept a commission as a major general in the Mexican army and to command the American volunteer forces; a group of emigrant-soldiers consisting of three infantry divisions, one cavalry division, and nine artillery batteries, was to be organized along the frontier; regulations of the United States Army would be followed in organizing the force; Schofield would name the officers of the corps; the Mexican government would determine the pay and bonuses; upon their discharge the volunteers would have the rights and privileges of Mexican citizens; the enlistment term was three years; the president of Mexico and the commander in chief of the corps could grant commissions; financial support of the group would come from a loan negotiated by the Mexican republic in the United States.⁴⁶

Meanwhile, General Grant had talked over the project with President Johnson who called a cabinet meeting for June 16 to discuss the matter. At the conference Grant pointed out the danger to the United States of the continued occupation of Mexico by French troops and advocated support of an expeditionary force. Seward agreed that the French had to go, but he opposed Grant's plan saying it would bring war between France and the United States. He maintained that by peaceful diplomacy the French troops could be removed from Mexico within six months. Other cabinet members expressed no objection to Grant's proposal, while the secretary of war offered to give Schofield a year's leave of absence to lead the expedition.⁴⁷ But the matter was left in abeyance until Schofield returned to Washington.

The next month Grant notified Sheridan that Schofield would be making an inspection tour along the Rio Grande, and he ordered him to place the large quantity of surplus arms and munitions "convenient to be permitted to go into Mexico if they can be got into the hands of the defenders of the only Government we recognize in that country." Grant added that he would soon be directed to discharge all the men who could be spared and reminded him that "existing orders permit discharged soldiers to retain their arms and accoutrements at low rates, fixed in order." ⁴⁸ About this time Romero, in a letter to his chief in the foreign ministry, said, "I believe that we can count him now as one of the best friends of our country," while to Juárez he wrote, "Grant could not do more if he were a Mexican." ⁴⁹

But the hypothetical expeditionary army was never mustered, and Schofield ended up in France rather than Mexico. This switch can be traced to Seward who opposed Grant's plan and who convinced Schofield that he should go to Paris and persuade Napoleon III to withdraw his troops from Mexico. Schofield later noted:

I had, on the one hand, full authority from the War Department and the general-in-chief of the army, given with the knowledge and consent of the President of the United States, to organize and equip an army for the purpose of driving the French out of Mexico, and on the other hand a request from the State Department to go to France and try by peaceful means to accomplish the same end.⁵⁰

General Schofield accepted the mission to France, but his influence there was limited. He returned to Washington a year later having accomplished one objective that Seward had in mind—his absence from the United States. Romero and Grant were so angry with Seward's frustrating their plan for armed intervention in Mexico that they attempted, secretly and unsuccessfully, to force him out of the cabinet.⁵¹

Meanwhile Seward initiated a series of notes to the French government about the removal of troops from Mexico. These protests, along with the growing menace of Bismarck's Prussia and French discontent with the costly Mexican venture, led Napoleon to re-

---

⁴⁴ *Ibid.*, pp. 296–298, 315–316.
⁴⁵ Sheridan, 1902: **2**: p. 216.
⁴⁶ Romero's authorization in Mexico, Legación, 1870–1892: **6**: pp. 121–124. Romero-Schofield contract in Iglesias Calderón, 1907: p. 28. See also Schofield, 1897: pp. 379–385.

⁴⁷ Mexico, Legación, 1870–1892: **5**: pp. 360–361; Welles, 1911: **2**: p. 317.
⁴⁸ Grant's letter of July 25, 1865, in Schofield, 1897: pp. 380–382.
⁴⁹ Romero to Ministro de Relaciones Exteriores, July 25, 1865, Mexico, Legación, 1870–1892: **5**: pp. 360–361; see also Smart, 1963: p. 339.
⁵⁰ Schofield, 1897: p. 383. For clarification of Seward's handling of the Schofield mission to France, see Wriston, 1929: pp. 780–788. See also Van Deusen, 1967: pp. 489–490.
⁵¹ Evans, 1870: p. 270.

call his foreign legion beginning in 1866. Withdrawal of French support foreshadowed the end of Maximilian's empire; as the Gauls retreated the Juaristas occupied the abandoned cities and forts. Finally in the last months of the war Emperor Maximilian was captured, courtmartialed, executed, and Juárez once again ruled from Mexico City. Romero later admitted that Seward's policy "was the best in the end, and accomplished its object without entailing on Mexico the curse which usually falls on nations who call in a more powerful neighbor to relieve them from a present danger. . . ."[52]

In the period between the end of the Civil War in the United States and the termination of the French intervention in Mexico, Romero continued efforts on behalf of his republic. As outlined above, these varied from fomenting propaganda to seeking foreign loans and purchasing military hardware. He continued to protest any reported American aid to French or Mexican imperial forces, and he encouraged Americans to emigrate to Mexico and become soldiers. With the triumph of the Mexican republicans in 1867, Don Matías submitted his resignation and prepared to return home. For his voyage the United States provided the coast guard vessel *Wilderness* which carried him from Charleston, South Carolina, to Veracruz, Mexico.[53] Before Romero left the United States, his friends gave him a testimonial banquet at Delmonico's restaurant in New York, the location of pro-Mexican meetings arranged by the Mexican minister in previous years. Following the meal many tributes were paid to the diplomat and the country he represented. Among the guests were William Cullen Bryant, Benjamin Holliday, William E. Dodge, Jr., Theodore Roosevelt, Sr., and four United States army generals.[54]

Romero's accomplishments in Washington during the French intervention were outstanding and of crucial importance to his government. Considering that he was in his twenties while dealing with much older men in a century and profession where age was highly respected, his labors take on additional value. In addition his health was poor; he suffered frequent epileptic attacks, migraines, kidney and stomach disorders.[55] Romero's importance was magnified between 1864 and 1867 because he was the only accredited diplomat representing the Mexican republic abroad. Nor were his diplomatic problems minor and easy to solve—the 1860's mark the Mexican republic's financial and political nadir. But as a distinguished American diplomatic historian has observed, "This remarkable man of prodigious industry and energy . . . seems to have been a master of the arts of personal politics,"

and he added that Romero had "an understanding of democratic institutions remarkable in a Mexican of the sixties. . . ."[56] General Grant's military aide and biographer, who was well acquainted with Romero, said of him:

No diplomatist has ever been accredited to this country who established more intimate relations with the important personages of the State; who appreciated better the national institutions and character; who played the legitimate *rôle* of a foreign minister with greater skill or success.[57]

Romero's achievements during this trying period are capped by his success in convincing leaders in the United States to recognize Juárez as head of the only legitimate government in Mexico. That recognition continued even though the itinerant nature of Juárez's government between 1863 and 1867 made it impractical to have a resident United States minister in the temporary capitals. In Washington the Mexican minister's ability to make friends with important leaders, including army generals and cabinet members, mark him as an outstanding diplomat, while his voluminous correspondence for that period—17,094 letters written and 11,172 letters received—reflects his professional diligence.[58] Another criterion of his success might be the hundreds of thousands of guns and millions of rounds of ammunition forwarded to Mexico by agents under Romero's control. The following chapters will give details about the activities of principal Mexican secret agents in the United States during the 1860's.

III. GENERAL VEGA—CALIFORNIA ARMS SMUGGLER

One of the most important of the secret agents sent to the United States by President Juárez was General Plácido Vega who operated out of San Francisco, California. During his two-and-a-half-year stay in California, General Vega initiated a number of projects, many of them clandestine, related to promoting the cause of the constitutional government of Mexico. But the paramount purpose of his mission was to procure arms and articles of war for the Juárez forces, and in spite of neutrality and arms-embargo laws he managed to ship thousands of rifles, millions of rounds of ammunition, and substantial quantities of other military supplies to Mexico.

General Vega's clever political support of California and Union leaders and issues as well as the financial transactions he negotiated mark him as an astute and capable emissary. In the course of his commission the Mexican agent disbursed $619,593.18 most of which

---

[52] *Ibid.*, p. 269.
[53] Mexico, Legación, 1870–1892: **10**: pp. 441–442.
[54] Guest list and speeches in Mexico, Legación, *Circulares,* 1868: **2**: pp. 358–392.
[55] Cosío Villegas, 1955–1965: **5**: p. 8.

[56] Perkins, 1933: p. 424.
[57] Badeau, 1888: p. 397.
[58] Tabular breakdown of Romero's correspondence in Abbot, 1869: pp. 183–184. See also Romero, 1898: p. ix.

was spent for military goods.[1] His account books show that in addition to arms purchases he distributed several thousand dollars to friendly San Francisco newspapers and allocated funds to frustrate pro-French filibustering expeditions. Vega also organized Mexican Clubs and Monroe Doctrine Societies throughout California and Nevada; these organizations raised men and money for the Mexican countermarch. In addition, the Mexican general opened a recruiting office in San Francisco where he enlisted American volunteers in the Mexican army.

Who was this Mexican secret agent that spent over half a million dollars in San Francisco between 1864 and 1866? Commissioner Plácido Vega was from the state of Sinaloa on Mexico's Pacific coast, and he, along with several members of his family, had risen to high offices in the state government. Although born and raised on the Rancho de Tecolua near the town of Fuerte, Don Plácido spent a number of years in the seaport city of Mazatlán.[2]

During the liberal-conservative civil war known as *La Reforma,* Vega sided with Comonfort, Lerdo de Tejada, and the other reformers. In fact, Vega was such a well-known liberal and supporter of that iconoclast Benito Juárez, that when Father Jesús Valdés married Plácido and his first cousin Clara in the Catholic church of Fuerte, the priest was punished by the conservative hierarchy—he became a *"cura sin parroquia."*[3] In August of 1858 Vega issued a *pronunciamiento* in favor of the liberal constitution of 1857 and, putting himself at the head of a body of troops, he marched off to meet and defeat a conservative military detachment. The following year Colonel Plácido Vega was named provisional governor of Sinaloa. In 1860 Vega again took to the field in command of the Sinaloa liberals, and in May of that year he celebrated another victory against the reactionary forces. On November 20, 1860, the Juárez government promoted Vega to the rank of general and gave him command of the Sinaloa Brigade.[4]

When the intervention war began with the arrival of European troops on Mexican soil, Governor Vega pledged a contingent of forces from his state for the unified national army. Most of 1862 was spent in outfitting and training the Sinaloa Brigade, but in February of the following year, Vega's army, over 2,000 strong, headed for the war front. Before boarding ship in Mazatlán, Vega addressed his troops, "Soldiers! The day which we have so anxiously de-

FIG. 2. General Plácido Vega, Mexican secret agent in California. Photo courtesy of the California Historical Society.

sired has arrived: that of initiating our march to take part in the glorious struggle."[5]

The Sinaloa Brigade arrived in Mexico City on March 31, 1863, having disembarked in Zihautenejo and marched overland via Acapulco and Chilpancingo. Following an interview with President Juárez, General Vega accepted command of the Third Division and moved his men to the Puebla war zone. On May 8, in the battle of San Lorenzo, Vega's troops were severely defeated by the French army and, after leaving the remainder of his brigade with General Porfirio Díaz, the Sinaloa commander returned to the capital for further orders.[6]

The subsequent surrender of Puebla to the French army forced Juárez to abandon Mexico City, and so Vega, along with the chief federal authorities, moved to San Luis Potosí. At this critical period there were intrigues against the Mexican president, but Vega appears to have been a loyal supporter of Juárez and the one who warned him of a planned *coup d'état.*[7]

In the temporary capital of San Luis Potosí the Juarist cabinet decided to send Vega abroad on a secret mission to procure arms. On July 5, 1863, Juan An-

---

[1] Statement of expenditures in Plácido Vega Papers, **13**, "Balance," Bancroft Library.

[2] According to a document in the Agustín Alviso Papers, Keith Ponsford Collection, Gen. Vega hypothecated Rancho de Tecolua to Agustín Alviso in 1866 as security for a $20,000 loan.

[3] Estrada Rousseau, 1952: p. 45.

[4] Buelna, 1924: pp. 48, 54, 60, 65.

[5] Estrada Rousseau, 1954: p. 15.

[6] Buelna, 1924: pp. 71–72; Bancroft, 1888: **6**: p. 66.

[7] Bancroft, 1888: **6**: pp. 72–73.

tonio de la Fuente, minister of foreign relations, issued confidential orders authorizing Vega to go to California or other points in the United States. His instructions specified that he was to purchase rifles, one or two machines for making guns, rifled cannon, and gunpowder, all of which were to be forwarded to Mexico with as much speed as possible. To pay for the war goods, General Vega was empowered to negotiate the receipts of the Mazatlán and Guaymas customhouses to the amount of $260,000. Of this amount $10,000 was specified to cover the personal expenses of the commissioner. Vega was also instructed to forward to Oaxaca the 1,000 guns deposited in Sinaloa which he had previously offered to the national government. Vega's credentials, signed by the ministers of war and foreign relations, stated that the bearer was charged with a high commission and commanded all Mexican citizens to render him every assistance possible.[8]

Foreign Minister Sebastián Lerdo de Tejada issued supplementary instructions to General Vega on September 10, 1863. They stated that a trustworthy report indicated that there were no guns or war goods available in California and suggested that he head directly for New York or other points specified in the previous orders. However, if Vega had reliable intelligence that the objects of his commission could be secured in San Francisco, he was free to go there. In case arms were to be sent from New York or other points on the Atlantic coast, preference was to be given to the overland route to Mexico via rail and dray line to Chihuahua. Although the sea route was faster, it was not as safe owing to the control and inspection of exports by United States authorities and the patrol of Mexican waters by the French navy. The codicil instructions closed with a recommendation that Vega begin his trip as soon as possible, and the foreign minister also noted that "among the similar commissions, that of yourself is the one in which the government puts its highest confidence."[9]

Upon receipt of his orders General Vega did not go to California immediately, instead he sent one of his aides. The assistant, Felipe de Arellano, arrived in San Francisco aboard the *Orizaba* on October 21, 1863.[10] Two months later Vega, writing to Arellano from Mazatlán, acknowledged receipt of 143 Colt pistols and 1,400,000 percussion caps. By the end of January, 1864, Arellano reported that he had sent 1,054 rifles in addition to earlier shipments.[11]

Finally on March 12, 1864, General Vega boarded the steamship *Oregon* at Mazatlán, and eight days later he along with 192 other passengers went ashore at San Francisco, California.[12] Accompanying Vega were several aides; two of them were Pedro G. Barraza and Juan José Ochoa, the latter sent along by José Patoní, the governor of Durango. Ochoa was instructed to conclude a proposed contract for arms with an unnamed American colonel at Mazatlán, and he was also to see whether Melchore Company had received a machine for making rifles and cannon, the machine to be operated by a four-horsepower steam engine. Ochoa was ordered to work with Vega in buying arms and he was to convey the munitions purchased back to Durango.[13]

From customhouse receipts at Mazatlán, Vega brought with him cash and letters of credit totaling $262,578.19.[14] But the Mexican commissioner had financial sources other than customs duties. For example there were loans and gifts from American sympathizers and businessmen as well as funds obtained from the sale of Mexican bonds. Vega also had authorization to dispose of certain Mexican islands and other national property, and the power to sell concessions for mining and exploitative ventures.

One of the revenue-producing leases negotiated by General Vega was for the salt deposits of Carmen Island which is situated in the Gulf of California. In 1864 the Carmen Island Salt Company was organized with offices in New York and San Francisco. The announced purpose of the corporation, capitalized at $250,000, was to lease the salt concession of Carmen Island and to transport the mineral to California and elsewhere for marketing. A company brochure, printed in Spanish and English editions, stated that the deposits contained over one hundred million cubic feet of salt located only 700 yards from the shore of Salinas Bay on the north side of the island. The pamphlet gave statistics of salt exports for previous years and tables indicating probable future sales and profits.[15] Besides Vega, the men involved in the company were Albert H. Osborn of San Francisco and New York; José María Aguirre de la Barrera, Mexican consul in San Francisco; and General Edward F. Beale, surveyor general of California. Vega later stated that he had obtained enough money from the Carmen Island lease to buy "some machines for making rifles as well as a quantity of armament."[16]

Soon after Vega's arrival in San Francisco he set up an office in Frank's Building on Portsmouth Square and proceeded to make confidential arrange-

---

[8] Original instructions in Plácido Vega Papers, **1**: fol. 9–11.
[9] Supplementary instructions, *ibid.*, fol. 28–31; a third set, dated March 30, 1864, reiterated earlier orders.
[10] Arellano to Vega, October 22, 1863, *ibid.*, fol. 107.
[11] Vega to Arellano, December 21, 1863 and Arellano to Vega, January 29, 1864, *ibid.*, fol. 346, 371–378.

[12] San Francisco *Alta California*, March 21, 1864: p. 1. Elsewhere Vega erroneously says he embarked at Mazatlan in April, Vega to McDowell, November 2, 1864, Plácido Vega Papers, **1**: fol. 768–782.
[13] Plácido Vega Papers, **1**: fol. 85–89.
[14] *Ibid*. **10**: fol. 334. According to Bancroft, 1888: **6**: p. 116, note 44, Vega brought $260,000 to California.
[15] Plácido Vega Papers, **1**: fol. 16; Spanish edition of the brochure in *ibid*. **3**: fol. 1.
[16] Vega to Beale, May 10, 1864, *ibid*. **1**: fol. 469.

ments and contracts in accordance with his commission. But he encountered troubles immediately.

Early in April, 1864, the San Francisco police chief and the port collector of customs seized 3,000 rifles which Vega had purchased and put aboard the American steamship *John L. Stephens*. This seizure of arms, like many others that followed, can be traced to the vigilance and bribery of the French consul in San Francisco, Charles de Cazotte. In his report to the French foreign minister, dated April 6, 1864, Cazotte said that after he was informed by a Frenchman that there were guns aboard the *John L. Stephens*, he "gave the information to the Collector of Customs and asked him to seize the shipment." The consul then added, "But here everything is done for money. The only way for me to succeed is to give money to certain agents, especially Chief of Police Burke who appears devoted to us." Subsequently Cazotte reported, "Today I paid Chief of Police Burke $200 (1,000 francs). Burke asked me to thank Your Excellency."[17] In addition to his office as chief of police, Edmund Burke was also a deputy collector of customs, a strategic location for a secret agent in the pay of the French government.

The San Francisco head collector of customs, Colonel Charles James, was sympathetic to the French position in Mexico, and he was on excellent terms with the French consul. Whether or not he received any "French gold," as Vega charged, Colonel James was adamant regarding arms shipments to Mexico by agents of Juárez. Legally, of course, he was in the right, for there was an embargo on arms shipments from the United States.

In July and August of 1864, acting on intelligence supplied by the French consul, Collector James and Chief of Police Burke frustrated one of the largest shipments of guns prepared by General Vega. This consignment comprised some 20,000 rifles, 18 cannon, ammunition and other military equipment which was to be conveyed to Mexico in two vessels that Vega had chartered. One ship, the *Haze*, was already loaded while the other, the *San Diego*, was preparing to take aboard the remainder of the cargo when an order was issued to confiscate all the arms until a bond was posted guaranteeing that they would not be exported from the United States.[18]

A provision of the embargo law permitted foreign arms to be reshipped to their point of origin, and since most of these guns had been sent from Hamburg, Germany, Vega declared that they were being returned to Germany via Liverpool. No doubt he had an agreement with the ship captains to drop the armament off in Mexico or transfer it to another ship at a high-seas rendezvous.

But Colonel James would not allow the arms to leave San Francisco—not even after Vega's friends Thomas Brown, special agent of the Treasury Department, and General Edward Beale, surveyor general of California, urged James to allow the shipment. Beale's letter was a particularly frank and emotional appeal:

I desire to talk to you very plainly as one citizen of a republic to another . . . who is about to lend his aid to the extinguishment of the last feeble flame of republicanism in a neighboring country. . . . You are known to have had frequent and cordial interviews with the consul of France, and you will be seen by the thoughtless multitude through a flood of French gold, which will be believed to have overwhelmed your integrity . . . I tell you that if these arms reach Mexico she will regain her liberties; but if, through the pusillanimous complaisancy of our government, by you, its agent, she should fall to the tender despotism of Austria, your name will become the synonym of everything that is humanly base wherever the Democracy rears the flag of a free people.[19]

Colonel James's reply to General Beale demonstrated that both of their inkwells contained similar acids. James said that "it was a mistake to suppose that the language of menace, contumely, and insult" would induce him to disregard his orders, and he added that he would not "connive at, promote, or cloak" any perjury. He also said, "My duty in the matter is plain and I can neither be bullied, wheedled, coaxed, or cajoled from performing it."[20]

In this difficult situation the *Haze* sailed without waiting for clearance papers, but it was overtaken at Half Moon Bay on August 5 and conducted back to San Francisco by revenue officials. The ship's cargo together with Vega's other arms deposits were taken to the United States arsenal at Benicia where they remained until they were sold at auction about a year later. The confiscated merchandise included the following boxes each containing 24 guns: 71 from the sloop *Haze*, 260 from the warehouse of Pacific Mail Steamship Company, 163 from #407 Battery Street, and 106 from #411 Sansome Street.[21] By December of 1864 the French consul was able to report to his home office that he was "responsible for the seizure of 14,000 guns and considerable military equipment."[22]

With reference to frustration of his plans and confiscation of his arms, General Vega accused the French consul of bribery and implicated several American officials. And it looked even worse for the United States officials when several subsequent episodes

---

[17] Cazotte to Drouyn de L'Huys, April 6, July 21, 1864, Archives du Ministère des Affaires Etrangères, Correspondence Politique des Consuls, Etats Unis, **19**: fol. 280–281 (microfilm), cited hereinafter as AAE/CPC.

[18] For a survey of this case and its aftermath see Frazer, 1946: pp. 391–399.

[19] Beale to James, July 16, 1864, Charles James Papers, fol. 14–18, Bancroft Library; see also Brown to James, July 16, 1864, *ibid.*, fol. 6–9. Their correspondence is printed in U.S. Congress, *House Exec. Doc. 73*, **2**: pp. 143–147.

[20] James to Beale, July 20, 1864, Charles James Papers, **1**: fol. 19–20.

[21] Seizure reported in *Alta California*, August 6, 1864.

[22] Cazotte to Drouyne de L'Huys, December 21, 1864, AAE/CPC, **19**: fol. 318–319.

seemed to confirm Vega's suspicion. In the case of the French warship *Rhin* that put into San Francisco Bay, Vega said it loaded supplies and took on men for the French Pacific squadron. He telegraphed Matías Romero, the Mexican minister in Washington, to protest the ambivalent American neutrality that aided France while denying the same assistance to Mexico. Romero asked the secretary of state to detain the *Rhin* until the alleged breach of neutrality could be investigated. In the end, the investigation of the case and the decision itself was left up to the San Francisco customs collector, Colonel James. After he was assured by the French consul and the captain of the *Rhin* that no arms would be taken aboard, he allowed the ship to sail.[23]

The following year in April, 1865, there was another protest by Vega and the Mexican consul about the use of California ports by French warships. The *Rhin* had been damaged in a storm off Mazatlán and was towed to San Francisco by the *Victoire,* flagship of the French Pacific squadron. The damaged French warship was repaired at the United States naval shipyard at Mare Island, and the Mexicans insisted that this was a breach of American neutrality.[24]

When the American Civil War ended and the embargo on arms was rescinded, federal officials in California continued to obstruct Vega's plans for transporting munitions to Mexico. In mid-1865 the Mexican general decided to convey his purchases overland in small units, partly because the Pacific coast ports of Mexico were generally controlled by French and imperial forces, and partly to avoid detection and confiscation by the San Francisco team of Cazotte, Burke, and James. But when the French consul heard of Vega's overland plans he complained to Colonel James and to General Irving McDowell, army commander of the Department of the Pacific. In August McDowell issued instructions to prohibit the passing of arms across the frontier, and on October 11, 1865, he issued General Orders No. 17 which prevented armed parties and arms from moving over the border. When the Mexican minister in Washington complained about McDowell's order, the case was turned over to the attorney general who rendered an opinion that the order was not "in conformity with any laws bearing on the subject." On December 8, 1865, General McDowell countermanded his previous orders, and Vega reported no seizures of arms shipments during the following year.[25]

In spite of laws forbidding export of arms, General Vega managed to send out six shipments by sea in the summer and fall of 1865, as well as a movement of 15,000 rifles with ammunition to the Colorado River frontier.[26] Vega's success as an arms smuggler can be judged from the list of shipments in table 1. This chart is only a partial record due to the illicit nature of the business; figures cited are from confidential records and reports of the Mexican secret agent and the French consul in San Francisco.

In addition to making arrangements for the purchase and shipment of arms to Mexico, General Vega also functioned as a propaganda agent in California. His account books and a report of the French consul indicate that he distributed over $4,000 to friendly San Francisco newspaper editors.[27] At that time there were three Spanish-language newspapers in San Francisco, *La Voz de Méjico* published by Pedro Mancillas, José María Vigil's *El Nuevo Mundo,* and *Eco del Pacífico* owned by E. Derbec, editor of several French newspapers. *El Nuevo Mundo* was set up and sustained by funds provided by General Vega, and along with *Voz de Méjico* the paper was pro-Juárez and anti-French. *Eco del Pacífico* reflected the views of its owner, opposing Union policy toward Mexico and favoring the establishment of an empire in that country with French protection.

French newspapers in San Francisco in the 1860's were *L'Union Franco-Américain, Courrier de San Francisco,* and *Echo du Pacifique.* Toward the close of the Civil War these newspapers continued their editorial opposition to United States foreign policy especially with regard to Mexico. When news of Lincoln's assassination and the simultaneous knife attack on Seward reached San Francisco, a mob went to the offices of anti-administration newspapers *Democratic Press, Newsletter, Monitor, Franco-Américain,* and in a few minutes wrecked the furniture and presses. However, the *Echo du Pacifique* was saved by Police Chief Burke and General Irwin McDowell and their reinforcements. As a result of the mob action and in view of public opinion, *Echo du Pacifique* was suspended by the authorities in April, 1865.[28]

General Vega previously had trouble with the *Eco del Pacífico* and its editor, and at one point the Mexican sued the Frenchman for libel. In November, 1864, the *Eco* alleged that a shipment of arms had been "denounced by one of those degraded individuals in the service of Don Plácido Vega, and with the consent of that gentleman." The article went on to say, "What the object of the assassin of Sinaloa was in taking that infamous step we do not yet know but perhaps it will be discovered at a later period." In the subsequent libel

---

[23] Frazer, 1946: pp. 392–393.

[24] Mexico, Legación, 1870–1892: **5**: pp. 202–203, 299.

[25] Speed to Seward, December 23, 1865, U.S. Congress, *House Exec. Doc. 73,* **2**: pp. 229–230; see also Plácido Vega Papers, **3**: fol. 19.

[26] Plácido Vega Papers, **2**: fol. 479–480; **3**: fol. 73–74; Bancroft, 1888: **6**: p. 181, note 38.

[27] José M. Vigil to Vega, November 1, 1864, Plácido Vega Papers, **1**: fol. 759; see also **6**: *comprobante* 44; Cazotte to Drouyn de L'Huys, May 29, 1865, AAE/CPC, **23**; fol. 270–274.

[28] Cazotte to Drouyn de L'Huys, April 21, 1865, AAE/CPC, **23**: fol. 253–254.

TABLE 1
Clandestine Arms Shipments from San Francisco Arranged by General Vega

Date	Ship	Cargo	Reference
1863			
Jan or Feb	LIVE OAK	Arms	FFO/CPC, XV, 120–123
March 15	J. M. CHAPMAN	*20 men and arms	FFO/CPC, XV, 120–123
Dec 3	(unknown)	143 pistols & ammunition	Vega MS, I, 346
1864			
Jan	HERMINE	*Arms for Sonora	FFO/CPC, XIX, 275–276
Feb	FANNY MAJOR	1054 rifles & ammunition	Vega MS, VI, comp. 43
April 4	JOHN L. STEPHENS	*300 rifles	FFO/CPC, XIX, 280–281
May	GUILLETTA	War material	Vega MS, I, 459, 467
June	(small boats)	Arms & naval stores	FFO/CPC, XIX, 286–287
June 10	POTTER	Arms & 2500 bbls. powder	FFO/CPC, XIX, 286–287
July 19	SAN DIEGO	*4992 guns	FFO/CPC, XIX, 288–289
Aug 5	HAZE	*3992 guns & ammunition	FFO/CPC, XIX, 293–294
Aug 18	W. L. RICHARDSON	$1403 freight paid	
Oct 9	METROPOLIS	$2500 freight paid	FFO/CPC, XIX, 312–313
1865			
Feb 20	SAN DIEGO	*Large amt. of arms	FFO/CPC, XXIII, 242
March 22	CONSTITUTION	528 rifles to Acapulco	FFO/CPC, XXIII, 255–256
May 20	ALERT	80 recruits & arms	FFO/CPC, XXIII, 278–279
May 20	BRONTES	*400 men; 6240 rifles	FFO/CPC, XXIII, 269–274
May 20	PONTIAC	*Men and arms	S. F. *Daily Call*, 5/23/'65
June	FANNY FREESBY	Arms c/o M. Ferrer	Vega MS, II, 480, 503
July 18	ELIZABETH OWENS	Arms & 3 officers	Vega MS, II, 470, 480, 503
Sept	GOLDEN CITY	*552 guns for Acapulco	FFO/CPC, XXIII, 344, 348
Sept 9	ELLA FLORENCE	3000 rifles	FFO/CPC, XXIII, 344, 348
Sept 16	JOHN & SAMUEL	3168 rifles & powder	Vega MS, II, 500, 514
Oct 14	ALERT	$2000 in arms	FFO/CPC, XXIII, 353, 354
Dec 4	FLYING DART	8000 rifles	Vega MS, III, 149
1866			
Jan	REINE POMARE	*9 boxes arms to Mazatlán	FFO/CPC, XXIX, 4, 5, 13
March	ARIZONA	Arms from San Diego	FFO/CPC, XXIX, 19–21
June 7	MARIA	Arms for Baja Calif.	FFO/CPC, XXIX, 72–73
July 5	(unknown)	863 rifles; 11,950 cartridges	AHMR, 2599, f. 11
July 8	KEOKA	7000 rifles & recruits	FFO/CPC, XXIX, 83–86
July 17	PACIFIC	Sent by Ant. Mancillas	Vega MS, II, 460
July 20	JOSEPHINE	Arms & recruits	FFO/CPC, XXIX, 85–86
Aug	HERMINIA	Arms c/o Captn. Gilbert	Vega MS, III, 523
Dec 12	MARIA	*Arms & men	FFO/CPC, XXIX, 107–113

*—Seized or frustrated by collector of customs & French consul.
Vega MS—Plácido Vega papers in Bancroft Library, Univ. of Calif.
FFO/CPC—French Foreign Office Archives, Correspondence Politique des Consuls, Etats Unis, microfilm, Bancroft Library.
AHMR—Archivo Histórico Matías Romero, Banco de México, México, D. F.

suit the Mexican agent won a moral victory and a $20 award.[29]

Working closely with Spanish newspapers of California, General Vega was able to organize patriotic juntas or Mexican Clubs throughout the state. These clubs, and those called Monroe Doctrine Societies, were very much more than platforms for patriotic oratory—they raised men and money for the Mexican defense effort. The clubs had a loose union with a general treasurer, and Vega was authorized by the local organizations to select his man for this key position.[30] Details of the contribution made by the Mexican Clubs can be seen in the reports to General Vega from club officers in Virginia City, Nevada; and Greenwood, Hornitos, Lancha Plana, La Porte, Los Angeles, Martinez, Marysville, New Almaden, Pinole, Sacramento, San Juan Bautista, San Francisco, San Pablo, Sonora, and West Point, California.[31] Mexican consul in San Francisco, Manuel Rodríguez, and his replacement, José A. Godoy, cooperated intimately with Vega and the Mexican Clubs.

Prominent in the activities of the Mexican Clubs were Californians of Spanish or Mexican descent, most of whom had been made United States citizens willy-nilly at the end of the Mexican War in 1848. Fifteen years

---
[29] Plácido Vega Papers, **1**: fol. 767 and **6**: *comprobante* 52.
[30] *Ibid.* **1**: fol. 637; see also fol. 616–636.
[31] *Ibid.*, fol. 615–695.

after the Treaty of Guadalupe-Hidalgo there were still many communities and ranchos in the West predominantly populated by Spanish-speaking people, and a residue of Mexicans remained influential in the social and political life of the former Mexican territory.

The Alviso, Castro, Pacheco, and Vallejo families, counted among the most notable and influential in northern California, sympathized with the Juárez government and gave moral and financial support to General Vega. On one occasion Augustín Alviso, Salvio Pacheco, Mariano G. Vallejo, and Victor Castro loaned Vega $24,000, and soon thereafter Melitón Alviso, Victor Castro, and Uladislao Vallejo sailed to Mexico in an armed company organized by Vega.[32] Another Pacheco family, important in the Santa Barbara region, also lent support to Vega. One member, Romualdo, the treasurer of the state of California, was an especially ardent supporter of the republican government of Mexico, and he arranged for several interviews between Vega and Governor Frederick Low and other state officials, as well as personally contributing money for the cause.[33] General Mariano Guadalupe Vallejo corresponded with General Vega, and the two men had several meetings in San Francisco and at Lachryma Montis, the Vallejo estate in Sonoma.[34] Don Augustín Alviso, who lived in Centerville, communicated with Vega soon after the general's arrival in San Francisco. The tone of his letter expresses the enthusiasm and warm reception given to the Mexican commissioner. Alviso wrote, "From the moment in which you arrived in this State, I have desired to see you and offer you my services with all the sincerity of a patriot . . . business pursuits have not permitted me to do it personally."[35]

Naturally, not all of the Mexicans living in California were of the same persuasion, and a number of them were apathetic about lending assistance to either the Juárez or the Maximilian faction. Sarmiento Blanco Villaseñor of Campo del Colorado, Mariposa County, lamented this condition when writing to General Vega. He was full of remorse and shame because his attempts to collect funds and to raise a company of soldiers had utterly failed. According to Blanco Villaseñor, it was as if a plague had scourged the land, for his Mexican neighbors were "heartless, without honor, and lacked love for their native land." He closed his letter with a plea for Vega to expand the propaganda campaign in order to arouse more sympathy and stimulate tangible aid for the republican regime. In a subsequent message Blanco Villaseñor announced that pride caused him to take up arms for the defense of Mexico.[36] A scathing denunciation of her fellow Mexicans was pronounced by a woman, Dolores Aros, of Jackson. In a letter to Vega she said that the indifference and lack of conscience of her compatriots were inexcusable, and she referred to the phlegmatic Mexicans as traitors.[37]

Cooperating with the Mexican minister in Washington, General Vega also used the Mexican Clubs to further the political ends of his government. For example, during the United States election campaign of 1864, the Mexican agent sent a printed circular to all the junta presidents urging them "for the salvation of the American Continent . . . to use all the influence possible . . . with the Hispanic Americans so that in the coming election of November 8 they will give their vote in support of the candidates of the republican party, for President Abraham Lincoln and Vice-President Andrew Johnson."[38] Vega was a vice-president of the San Francisco Central Union Club, and he donated a considerable amount of time to party activities. One receipt in the secret agent's file is for $178 contributed to the Union party coffers on November 1, 1864.[39]

Spanish-American residents of San Francisco formed their own Union club and pledged themselves to labor actively for the party candidates. The organization meeting was held at Philharmonic Hall, corner of Stockton and Jackson streets, on October 9, 1864. A newspaper report of the meeting noted that the walls of the hall were decorated with American, Mexican, Peruvian, and Chilean flags. A Peruvian, A. D. Spivalo, was chosen president of the group, which numbered over seventy members, and one of the major addresses was given by Ramón de Zaldo, an aide of General Vega. After the speeches and numerous *vivas* for "Lincoln, Liberty, American Independence, and Death to Despotism," the club adjourned.[40]

On Columbus Day of 1864 the Spanish American Union Club met again at the same place and heard several speeches by Latin American orators. Mr. J. M. Ainsa's discourse was typical:

Why is it that the party which represents the American government now asks the vote of the Spanish Americans? It is well known that in times past the dominant party in Washington has been hostile to Mexico; has hunted up causes of quarrel with the Spanish American republics; has threatened to conquer all the remainder of the continent, and extend slavery over it; and has favored filibusterism. With such a party no true republican ought to sympathize . . . the Union party is . . . against prejudices of color and race, against conquest, against foreign intervention, and against monarchical government on this continent.[41]

---

[32] *Ibid.* **4**: *Libro Mayor,* fol. 12; **3**: fol. 439, 687.
[33] Vega to Pacheco, November 21, 1864, *ibid.* **2**: fol. 24; see also **6**: *comprobante* 51, fol. 7.
[34] Vallejo to Vega, September 4, 1865, March 29, 1868, *ibid.* **2**: fol. 496; **3**, fol. 660.
[35] Alviso to Vega, August 17, 1864, *ibid.* **1**: fol. 591.
[36] Blanco Villaseñor to Vega, March 1, June 6, 1865, *ibid* **2**: fol. 260, 402.
[37] Aros to Vega, October 20, 1864, *ibid.* **1**: fol. 655.
[38] *Ibid.,* fol. 615.
[39] *Ibid.* **6**: *comprobante* 49; see also **1**: fol. 721, 725, 726.
[40] *Alta California,* October 10, 1864.
[41] *Ibid.,* October 13, 1864.

On the same evening General Vega attended a Mexican Club meeting in Sacramento where he supported the Union candidates. In an eloquent speech the Mexican general portrayed the wrongs inflicted on Mexico by the French and their puppet emperor, Maximilian, and the meeting closed with a series of resolutions protesting the French attempt to subjugate Mexico and pledging support for Lincoln and Johnson.[42] Letters to the San Francisco *Alta California* during the weeks preceding the election gave further proof that many native Californians supported Lincoln. On page one of the October 21, 1864, *Alta* it is noted that "Late letters from the Southern Coast Counties say that the Union Party will gain many votes at the next election among the Spanish Americans who sympathize with Juárez and hate Maximilian and his friend Jeff Davis." It was natural that Vega and other partisans of the republican government of Mexico would support Lincoln since his administration officially recognized Benito Juárez as the legitimate head of the Mexican nation and refused to recognize Maximilian or treat with any of his emissaries. For a Latin American government, recognition by the United States was then, as now, an important requisite for success. In addition several powerful men in Lincoln's camp supported Juárez; some of them openly favored sending troops to drive the French army out of Mexico as soon as the Civil War in the United States was terminated.

But in spite of suggestions and plans in Washington, armed forces of the United States were not ordered across the Rio Grande. True, several thousand American adventurers and ex-soldiers crossed over to Mexico and joined the armies of Juárez and Maximilian. Some armed units were organized in the United States by Mexican secret agents and transported to Mexico where they fought together although attached to Mexican armies. Among the American volunteers were a number of Californians recruited by Plácido Vega who paid their expenses, furnished their equipment, and made arrangements for their transportation to Mexico. The story of these soldiers of fortune will be considered in the following chapter.

IV. VEGA'S VOLUNTEER ARMY

General Plácido Vega, the Mexican secret agent sent to California in 1864, worked diligently to recruit men in San Francisco for the Mexican republican army. Two of the largest contingents that Vega organized were those he called the *Brontes* and *Keoka* expeditions, named after the principal ships chartered to carry the men to Mexico's Pacific coast. The first large group of about four hundred men was assembled during the closing months of the Civil War when existing laws prohibited the export of arms and the departure of armed parties from the United States. To circumvent neutrality and emigration laws the *Brontes* group was officially known as the Arizona Exploring Expedition and the volunteers were called colonists. Since there were hostile Apache Indians along the border at that time, emigrants had good reason to be well armed. But in spite of justifications and terminology, the real destination of the armed colonists was always clear to Vega and to the recruits—they were a military expeditionary force bound for the battle lines of Mexico.[1]

All during his stay in San Francisco the Mexican general received letters from men who wanted to join Juárez's military forces. As might be expected, a great many of the volunteers were Californians of Spanish or Mexican descent, many of whom were still more oriented toward Mexico City than Washington, D. C. Unquestionably some of those who wrote to the Mexican agent were sincere patriots and idealists who wanted to see a republican government restored in that land. Others expressed their hatred of the French violation of the Monroe Doctrine, and they indicated that they were willing to fight for that principle. Many of the volunteers had seen recent service in the War of the Rebellion where they had served one-, two-, or three-year enlistment periods. Some applicants had been discharged as a result of wounds received in battle; others were still in the United States services but expected early separation as their terms of enlistment were fulfilled and as the end of the war drew near. When the Civil War finally ended in April, 1865, the volume of letters to General Vega increased tremendously as did the number of men who called on him at his office on Portsmouth Square.

Most of the American volunteers requested commissions as officers and other incentives to join the Mexican army; several applicants offered to raise a company of men, others agreed to furnish their own arms, ammunition, and horses. One volunteer, Edward A. Lever, crossed the entire American continent to make himself available for service in the Mexican army according to his letter from San Francisco dated November 4, 1864. Lever said that after his arrival in California friends tried to dissuade him from his course; he went on to say, "Being in heart and soul a believer in republicanism, I have long sympathized with Mexico and her patriots, therefore I offer myself for any position whereby I might be of service to the sister republic of my own dear native country."[2] In subsequent letters to General Vega he wrote:

I can raise a company of thoroughbred Americans, many of whom have seen service in the East and have been comrades in arms with myself.

Will you accept a company of good men? Equip them? Commission their officers and furnish them with means of transportation to where you may need them?

If you will do this, all I have to ask is that the company

---

[42] *Sacramento Daily Union*, October 12, 1864.

[1] Pamphlets and correspondence about the Arizona Exploring Expedition in Plácido Vega Papers, **6**: *comprobante* 51.

[2] Lever to Ramón de Zaldo, *ibid.* **1**: fol. 818.

will have a chance to prove what they are against the foreign and domestic hordes that acknowledge the sway of the usurper.

You know the courage, dash and endurance of American soldiers. We will provide for ourselves and for many more besides. Maximilian shall be our quartermaster and commissary. . . . I wish each French soldier was provided with two muskets for then we would be able to take more from them. . . . I have little fear of the French for my countrymen have too often beaten the conquerors of the French to care much for them in a military point of view.[3]

After a personal interview with General Vega, Lever wrote a third letter in which he declared that the necessity of conversing through an interpreter was the cause of any lack of understanding between them. Arguing that an all-American military expedition to Mexico was a necessity, Lever said that many unemployed men in San Francisco would join such a unit. Other opportunities for energetic, ambitious young men, according to Lever, were to seek their fortune in the eastern states, to depart for China, to join the United States Army, or to sign on merchant ships sailing to other parts of the world. He added, "When my country sees that as many of her citizens are enlisted in this cause, interest and national pride will cause her to be more lenient towards your government."[4]

From Austin, Nevada Territory, a civil engineer, A. D. Rock, wrote to General Vega and estimated that a regiment could be raised if he were so authorized. He questioned the legality and feasibility of such an undertaking upon learning that a similar expedition led by H. A. Crabb had been apprehended by United States forces. Consequently, he had written to General Irwin McDowell, commanding officer of the Department of the Pacific, to ascertain whether the United States government would object to armed emigrants leaving the country. He proposed to go directly to Mexico through the Apache Indian country. Rock was originally a Virginian, and in a subsequent letter to Vega he expressed his sympathy for the plight of the Confederate states:

There seems to be an implied understanding between yourself and authorities of the United States that none shall be allowed to go to Mexico except those known to be opposed to the Southern States of our union. . . .

I believe for one that the Southern people, even many who may have been forced or drawn into the Rebellion, are as cordially sympathizing with Mexico in her troubles as are other people, and that they desire to go there for the purpose of acting the part of good citizens without any reference to the late trouble of the United States. . . . I, sir, have been doing all in my power to strengthen the aims of President Juárez in sustaining the true and rightful government; but if any arrangement is made as to what class of men may leave our ports, then indeed I have been working in vain.[5]

Several other residents of Nevada Territory wrote to General Vega inquiring about military service in Mexico. One was Daniel E. Hungerford of Virginia City, a veteran of the Mexican War, Indian campaigns, and a former regimental commander in the Army of the Potomac, who requested authority and inducements to raise an armed company. A postscript to his message said that, if joining the Mexican forces entailed compromising the government of the United States, or favoring the recognition of the Southern Confederacy, he could not countenance the movement nor participate in it.[6]

Meanwhile, in San Francisco General Vega's headquarters was besieged by applicants and adventurers. S. G. George, a physician and surgeon, had made several unsuccessful attempts to secure an interview with the Mexican agent according to his letter from San Francisco dated December 9, 1864. He wanted the usual information about pay and bonuses for military service with the republican forces. On the same day and in the same city two veterans of the Union army, William H. Tuttle and C. W. Harris, wrote to Vega and requested an interview for the following morning. James Armstrong, a prospective emigrant, arrived at Vega's office with a letter of introduction from A. J. Bryant, president of the Union Club of San Francisco. In the words of Bryant his candidate was well qualified, for besides being a veteran of the United States Army, "whose service he only left when dangerously wounded," Armstrong was a capable politician having served in the recent successful Republican presidential campaign.[7]

In the late summer of 1864 Vega commissioned Francisco Warner of San Francisco as a lieutenant colonel in the Mexican army. When his pay was not forthcoming, and after four weeks of receiving the *mañana* response from Ramón de Zaldo, one of Vega's assistants, Warner wrote the Mexican commissioner:

If it was not convenient for you to let me have the money I would have been far better satisfied had you told me. But if you wish to redeem your promise you can do so by sending the money to the fruit store cor. Dupont and Sutter Sts. this week or I shall be obliged to accept aid from another source. I can serve the Imperial party and they know it or they would not have offered me money to join them. . . .[8]

Two Spanish language newspapers of San Francisco, *La Voz de Méjico* and *El Nuevo Mundo*, the latter set up and sustained by funds provided by General Vega, published the official statements of the Juárez government and the inducements offered to emigrant soliders. The editors, Antonio Mancillas and José María Vigil, forwarded to Vega inquiries they received from prospective soldiers. One such message was from Francisco Catalán of Sutter Creek who requested information for himself and three friends about an announced force of

---

[3] Lever to Vega, November 15, 21, 1864, *ibid.* **2**: fol. 18, 25.

[4] Lever to Vega, November 21, 1864, *ibid.*, fol. 25.

[5] Rock to F. F. Gallardo, July 1, 1864; Rock to Vega, May 19, 31, 1865, *ibid.* **1**: fol. 511; **2**: fol. 362, 385.

[6] Hungerford to Vega, July 16, 1864, *ibid.* **1**: fol. 533; see also fol. 562 and **2**: fol. 373, 376.

[7] George to Vega and Harris to Vega, December 9, 1864; Bryant to Vega, May 18, 1865, *ibid.* **2**: fol. 110, 197, 361.

[8] Warner to Vega, October 25, 1864, *ibid.* **1**: fol. 735.

Americans headed for Mexico overland through Arizona Territory. Twenty-five or thirty reprints of articles in *La Voz de Méjico* and some pamphlets in English outlining the pay and bonus schedule for volunteer soldiers were requested by A. L. Cervantes of San Luis Obispo. He promised that the printed matter would be widely circulated in that area.[9]

Some men who were then serving in the United States armed forces were interested in the opportunities for soldiering in Mexico. Captain H. C. Flynn, who addressed several letters to Vega, spoke for himself and ten or twelve others with military qualifications who were eager to join the Mexican army. In his letters from San Francisco he inquired about the incentives promised to United States officers who would go to Mexico. Flynn stated that he disavowed the infamous term adventure; he and his friends wanted to serve the cause of an independent Mexico. In one letter Flynn also offered to furnish a bodyguard to the Mexican general. Marked confidential, one letter came from the Presidio of San Francisco, and the writer, Lieutenant Montgomery Maze, Second Infantry Regiment, California Volunteers, designated himself a solider of fortune eager to participate in the Mexican conflict. An assistant surgeon in the same regiment, F. M. Cassill, asked about inducements for medical men who wanted to go to Mexico. He added, "I have always had a lively interest in the fate of our sister republic ever since the Frenchman's foot first polluted her soil."[10]

From other military posts in the San Francisco area messages were forwarded to Vega. Thomas Fellows, Company A, Sixth Infantry, stationed on Alcatraz Island in San Francisco Bay, spoke for himself and several comrades. These men had been real soldiers of fortune; their military commitments had taken them to Nicaragua, Costa Rica, and New Granada. Four months remained of their enlistment terms, and they wished no idleness at its conclusion. James B. Plunket of the United States Navy, Second Aft Engineer aboard the ironclad U.S.S. *Comanche,* wrote to the Mexican emissary from Mare Island Navy Yard. Plunket had previously served two years as a captain of infantry volunteers in the Army of the Potomac. He said that, "as the war is virtually ended, and my services will not be required much longer, it is my desire to resign and enter the Mexican Army."[11]

Mining camps in the Sierra Nevada of California proved to be a fertile source of manpower for the projected expeditions to Mexico. The Mexican Clubs organized by Vega were centers for the dissemination of information and in some places coordinated the recruitment and training of volunteers. In Jackson, Amador County, Juan de la Fuente distributed propaganda leaflets and posted newspaper editorials throughout the region. And in nearby San Andreas a Mexican, Joaquín Miranda Viña, noted that he had read some of the newspaper articles to himself and several friends, and they desired to join one of the Mexican-bound expeditions. A fortnight later he wrote that three men, Precipiano Morillo, Frederico Robinson, and Cuaristo Nuñez were ready to depart for San Francisco. Certain that his letter would reach General Vega before the men, he warned that they would arrive financially destitute and wanted the general to be on guard. A different form of voluntary aid was tendered by two Grass Valley men. George B. Shearer and Charles J. Miller wrote, "We are both practical printers and desire to assist you in your endeavors to drive from your dearly beloved country your deadly enemy." They offered to help the republican cause by means of the written and printed word, and also inquired about the need for printers on Mexico's west coast.[12]

The quicksilver mining district around New Almaden had a large Spanish surname population, and a number of letters to General Vega were posted from that city. Gregorio López, who worked in the mines, was a native of Sinaloa, and he volunteered to return to his besieged homeland in one of the expeditions being formed. López offered to serve as a guide and pack train muleteer. Avowing that "literacy and patriotism are not inseparable companions," he had a friend, Crecencio Avalos, write his letter to Vega. An officer in the Mexican Club of New Almaden, Romualdo Velásquez, wrote a letter of introduction for a Chilean volunteer, Señor Villalón, in which he pointed out that his candidate was known by Señor Sepúlveda, an acquaintance of Vega. Another letter of introduction to Vega was presented by Eduardo Segura. The writer was Jesús Herrera of New Almaden, and the note contained the usual laudatory commendation.[13]

Juan Días, who lived in San Jose, reported that after he had volunteered to go to Mexico, he "encountered some family difficulties." He suggested that all would be well if Vega would allow Señora Días to accompany the expedition. And from Marysville, Vega heard that a native California infantry company had been raised with the ultimate objective of aiding Juárez. The correspondent requested a Spanish book on military tactics so that his contingent could be adequately prepared. The letter was signed by José Buentello Elizando and included the name of Dr. Lorenzo Hubbard to whom the requested volume was to be sent.[14]

---

[9] Catalán to Mancillas, May 14, 1865; Cervantes to Vega, May 20, 1865, *ibid.* 2: fol. 342, 366.

[10] Flynn to Vega, June 28, July 10, 1864; Maze to Vega, May 8, 1865; Cassill to Vega, June 20, 1865, *ibid.* 1: fol. 526, 528; 2: fol. 336, 414.

[11] Fellows to Vega, June 2, 1865; Plunket to Vega, June 11, 1865, *ibid.* 2: fol. 394, 407.

[12] de la Fuente to Vega, May 21, 1865; Miranda Viña to Vega, May 20, June 5, 1865; Shearer and Miller to Vega, June 2, 1865, *ibid.,* fol. 365, 367, 397, 398.

[13] Avalos to Vega, May 14, 1865; Velásquez to Vega, May 24, 1865; Herrera to Vega, June 5, 1865, *ibid.,* fol. 344, 375, 396.

[14] Díaz to Vega, June 3, 1865; Elizando to Vega, March 22, 1865, *ibid.,* fol. 395, 275.

General Vega did not limit his activities to signing up the many American volunteers; he actively recruited men and advertised inducements offered by his government to solider-colonists. President Juárez, pushed out of central Mexico by the French armies, had promised high military pay and large land bonuses to foreigners who would emigrate to Mexico and fight against the invaders. Vega, Matías Romero, and the other Mexican agents in the United States distributed thousands of copies of a pamphlet entitled *Decrees of the Mexican Constitutional Government Inviting American Emigrants to Settle in the Republic*. A few of the statements in it about the wonders of Mexico and the advantages of settling there are worth noting:

> Mexico is the finest country in the world. There a person may enjoy every kind of temperature that he may desire. There is abundance of water to irrigate the soil. Mexico only needs peace to be able to afford the means of enjoying all the luxuries of a happy life.
> In conclusion, this fine country offers such advantages to the industrious and persevering settler that, in a short period of time he could not fail to acquire a more comfortable and easy homestead than can be had in any other part of the world with the same amount of labor.[15]

The pamphlet also listed the Mexican army salaries and gave details about the land bonus for veterans.

No doubt the material concessions and military opportunities outlined in the pamphlet induced A. A. C. Williams of San Francisco, a former colonel who had served three years as a surgeon in the United States Army, to address General Vega volunteering his services to Mexico. Williams was in California recovering from a Civil War wound, and he accompanied his letter of April 5, 1865, with documentary evidence of his service and testimonials from Generals Hooker, Rinney, Richardson, Berdan, and Jackson. He qualified his offer of service to Mexico with a statement concerning the commission he would accept:

> The rank which I have held in the United States Service during the war, that of Colonel, precludes my accepting even temporarily any position with a lower rank. At the same time I would respectfully urge my claims for a commission as a Brigadier General from the President of the Republic of Mexico believing myself fully competent in every respect for the responsibilities incident to that rank.[16]

General Vega was quite impressed with Williams; within a week he commissioned him a colonel in the Mexican national guard. At the same time he forwarded the request of Colonel Williams for a general's rank to the Mexican government. About a month later Vega promoted Williams to brigadier general in the Mexican army.[17]

During March, April, and May of 1865 Vega made plans to send two large expeditions of armed colonists to Mexico. He rented an office at 127 Montgomery Street, San Francisco, as an enlistment center for soldier-colonists, and in April he put Williams in charge. Vega spent these months locating men, munitions, and money. He wrote to many of the men who had applied earlier outlining plans for the Arizona Exploring Expedition and sending along some of the emigration pamphlets. Recruits were even solicited among California prisoners who were serving short sentences. Vega sent a package of propaganda leaflets with a letter to San Quentin prisoner Ernest C. Roland and asked that the printed matter be circulated among the "loyal and enthusiastic defenders of our sacred cause."[18]

Through the Mexican Clubs, General Vega had agents in a number of California cities to whom letters and telegrams were dispatched urging volunteers to organize and proceed to San Francisco. The men were to sail in two components, the first on May 13 and the second one twelve days later. From Marysville, Sacramento, Vallejo, San Jose, Petaluma, and other cities came favorable replies. Romualdo Velásquez promised eighty to one hundred men from New Almaden, twenty-five of whom could be mustered in two hours. As a complimentary gesture the citizens of that mining town forwarded a shotgun and a pistol to General Vega.[19]

A letter from Virginia City, Nevada Territory, stated that insufficient funds for transportation was all that hindered a group of two hundred volunteers from coming to San Francisco. The writer, Donaciano Mazón, told of the enthusiastic pro-Mexican support in that area. Juan de la Fuente of Jackson, California, announced that an emigrant party was ready to depart for Mexico. He reported that the group was composed of Chileans, Mexicans, and other Spanish Americans; the men were from Jackson, Sutter Creek, Dry Town, Fiddletown, and Volcano. The correspondent regretted that he could not join the patriotic band and gave as his excuse, "extreme poverty plus an old father and mother and six little brothers and sisters."[20]

Specific details concerning embarkation of the troops were forwarded to detachment leaders by letter, telegram, and messenger. Several Sonoma volunteers, including one of General Vallejo's sons, Uladislao, were notified of the plans. Francisco Ramonet of Sacramento was ordered to bring his men to the port, and State Treasurer Pacheco reported from the capital, "The Americans are going to you in a group for their security. There is not an hour to lose. Let me know the time of

---

[15] Copy of pamphlet in *ibid.* **3**; fol. 429; see pp. 10–11 of pamphlet.
[16] Williams to Vega, April 5, 1865, *ibid.* **6**; *comprobante* 51, fol. 5.
[17] Vega to Williams, April 11, 1865, *ibid.*, fol. 6.
[18] Vega to Roland, May 11, 1865, copy in AAE/CPC, **23**: fol. 317–318.
[19] Velásquez to Vega, May 7, 1865, Plácido Vega Papers, **6**: *comprobante* 51, fol. 13; Ochoa to Vega and Salmon to Vega, May 12, 1865, *ibid.* **2**: fol. 337.
[20] Mazón to Vega, May 18, 1865; de la Fuente to Vega, May 21, 1865, *ibid.* **2**: fol. 356, 367.

sailing. Probably tomorrow I shall come down to the city."[21]

One of the officers of the Arizona Exploring Expedition, W. H. Lewis, was informed that he could go as a major with the first contingent, although Vega preferred that he should go with the second battalion as a colonel. Lewis, who was in San Francisco, replied by note, "General, I am willing to do as you think best, but my heart is with your cause and I am anxious to go."[22]

Meanwhile, General Vega was trying to raise money for the venture. He had certain funds derived from customhouse receipts at Mazatlán and Guaymas as well as credits in San Francisco with import-export firms. But because there was not enough ready cash, Vega pawned jewelry belonging to members of his family for $3,200 in gold coin. A wealthy Californian, Don Vicente Ortiz, advanced the money, and the jewels guaranteed the loan which carried an interest rate of two per cent per month. An invoice of the precious stones, dated March 19, 1865, contains some twenty-six items including a lady's comb with 24 diamonds and an amethyst, a gold ring with 13 diamonds and 7 opals, a pair of gold earrings with 22 diamonds, and a pair of gold buttons with 22 pearls.[23]

General Vega turned over to General Williams $4,060 for the organization and outfitting of the American brigade, and another of Vega's agents, Juan Argos, spent $3,573.98 for supplies to be used by the expedition. The itemized expenses of these functionaries contain the following articles: canteens, mess kits, cloth for flags, lamps, iron pots, bacon, sugar, gun-powder, and one cannon.[24] The receipts show that some of the munitions were purchased from A. J. Plate, a San Francisco gunsmith.

Vega gave Williams an extensive set of military orders, instructions, letters of introduction to President Juárez and the members of his cabinet, and credentials which he could present to various Mexican state governors and military commandants along the route. His official orders read:

> In virtue of the powers and authority which the supreme government of the Constitutional Republic of Mexico has conferred on me, I give you full and ample powers in order that the number of colonists that will go from the U.S. to Mexico will be able to establish themselves at a place where they can better take advantage of the resources and elements. You will augment the number as much as possible, maintaining resolutely the best order, discipline and organization. You can in virtue of this power dispose of whatever interests, public or private, that may be necessary for the expedition in Mexican territory, giving the respective receipts to the interested and keeping the accountability required in these cases.

Also I authorize you to solicit in the U.S. loans, food, effects, and as many articles as you need for the circumstances.[25]

Finally, in May of 1865 about 400 colonists were ready to sail in two groups. The sailing ship *Brontes* was engaged, and payment of $1,255 was advanced to its master. Just as the first group was about to put to sea on May 20, a Coast Guard ship, the *Shubrick*, anchored alongside, and an officer ordered the *Brontes* to remain in port. The trouble seemed to be that the customs office in San Francisco objected to the munitions aboard the ship being sent to Mexico. It was true that, during the Civil War, President Lincoln had ordered that no arms or munitions were to be exported from the country, but on May 3, 1865, President Johnson revoked the order, and on May 15 the military headquarters, Department of the Pacific, published General Orders No. 37 which acknowledged the free export of arms. Actually General Williams had an order from the quartermaster general of the Department of the Pacific, stating that he could leave with armed men.[26] But the Treasury agents, the Port Collector of Customs, and the Coast Guard had not received official word of the lifting of the arms embargo, and they held up the expedition.

The French consul in San Francisco, Charles de Cazotte, had more than a little to do with this surveillance and detention of the *Brontes*. Naturally he was interested in preventing aid from reaching the Juárez forces, the latter being engaged in war against French troops in Mexico. Cazotte's complicity in the *Brontes* affair is borne out in his dispatches to the French Foreign Office and corroborated by contemporary newspaper accounts. Cazotte took credit for initiating the detaining action when he telegraphed the Foreign Ministry in Paris, "Upon my demand, vessel *Brontes,* having on board 400 military recruits and large armament for Mexico, was stopped by the authorities."[27]

A more detailed account of the French consul's officious intervention is available in the San Francisco *Daily Call* for May 23, 1865. There one reads that on May 20 Cazotte called on Mr. Phillips, the deputy port collector (Collector Charles James being out of the city), and protested the sailing of the *Brontes*. Phillips is reported to have said, "I can't see the point of your interference. This is a matter between the government of the U.S. and Maximilian. Neither the English or Dutch consul have been here to protest . . . and I can't see that you, as consul for France are any more concerned." The article adds that having had no success with Mr. Phillips, Cazotte then went to see Edmund Burke, Special Deputy Collector, from whom he obtained an order to have the vessels *Brontes* and *Pontiac* detained until advice from the

---

[21] Vega to Ramonet and Vega to Vallejo, May 10, 1865; Pacheco to Vega, May 16, 1865, *ibid.,* fol. 195; **6**: *comprobante* 51, fol. 23-24.

[22] Lewis to Vega, May 14, 1865, *ibid.* **2**: fol. 341.

[23] *Ibid.* **6**: *comprobante* 51, fol. 53.

[24] *Ibid.,* fol. 62, 65.

[25] *Ibid.,* fol. 57.

[26] Vega to Romero, June 30, 1865, *ibid.,* fol. 47.

[27] Telegram, Cazotte to Drouyn de L'Huys, San Francisco, May 24, 1865, AAE/CPC, **23**, fol. 269 *verso*.

Treasury Department in Washington. As was noted in the previous chapter, Burke was a secret agent in the pay of the French government.

General Vega was well aware of the harassing activities of Consul Cazotte. As early as October, 1863, one of Vega's agents in San Francisco, Felipe Arellano, reported, "The French consul is very astute, he has a secret police." In a letter to the Mexican minister in Washington, Vega acknowledged the counteraction of the French consul by saying, "One sees that the hand and gold of France and her petty officers are the cause of all these troubles."[28]

This was just the beginning of misadventure that was to curse the expedition for the next two months. In fact, ill fortune and adverse events were of such intensity that the Arizona Exploring Expedition never did sail from San Francisco, and some of the men including General Williams spent a number of days in jail on charges ranging from violation of neutrality laws to piracy. After the customs officials enforced their arms embargo, the munitions were removed and permission was asked for the emigrants to sail unarmed. This was not approved, and about 200 members of the detachment returned to their homes while approximately 150 remained on board the *Brontes* determined to emigrate if permitted.

Amid all this confusion General Williams and some of the other leaders of the expedition were arrested at one o'clock in the morning of May 24 on the charge of violating neutrality laws. They were later released on bail, but not until June 14 were they acquitted of this charge.[29]

In the meantime, new troubles beset Williams and twenty-one other members of the brigade. On May 25 they were arrested, jailed, and charged with conspiring to steal and carry away a steamboat, the *Colon*, in the harbor of San Francisco. This vessel was under the Peruvian flag and valued at $40,000. The complaint stated that, after the revenue ship *Shubrick* was ordered to watch the movements of the *Brontes*, a plan was formed to capture the *Colon*, take her behind Angel Island, and slip out the Golden Gate in the early hours of the morning. The *Alta California* for May 26, 1865, commented that, "The *Colon* was not coaled for a voyage, and the whole scheme—if such was formed—smacks of lunacy." Regardless of the opinion of editors about the case, the accused men found themselves in jail and awaiting trial. A few of them, including General Williams, Colonel Daniel E. Hungerford, and Lieutenant W. W. Bruce, were released on bail of $2,000 each.[30] One of the prisoners submitted the following epic poem, published in the *Alta California*, June 2, 1865:

---

[28] Arellano to Vega, October 22, 1863, Vega to Romero, June 30, 1865, Plácido Vega Papers, **1**: fol. 197; see also **6**: *comprobante* 51, fol. 47.

[29] *Alta California*, May 25, June 15, 1865.

[30] *Ibid.*, May 26, 1865.

'Twas on a Wednesday evening
  On the twenty-second of May,
That Chief Burke came, with his bold band,
  And carried us away!

On board the old barque *Brontes*,
  We'd just laid down to rest,
When there appeared a vision
  With a breast-pin on his breast!

He invited us to go on deck,
  Which we, of course, *did* do;
When, from among our number,
  Chief Burke picked twenty-two!

He called us "Williams' Pirates,"
  Which we thought mighty tall;
Then formed us into column
  And marched to City Hall!

With dignity commanding,
  Chief Burke did us then tell,
That *ten* from out our number
  He'd furnish with a cell!

We soon will have our trial,
  We feel that we'll be free!
We GLORY in our NOBLE cause-
  The fight for LIBERTY!!!!

We've ONE, at least, among our band,
  That's done HIS DUTY WELL;
He's battled for his Country's Flag,
  But *now lies in a cell!!*

Is this the gratitude he gets?
  Oh! no! it cannot be!
The Soldier of America
  Shall ever yet be FREE!!!!

                          BRONTES PRISONER, Cell No. 5

The *Brontes-Colon* affair came to trial in San Francisco's police court on June 5, 1865. The defense attorney, Judge Campbell, called no witnesses; instead he attacked the testimony of the prosecution deponents claiming that they had failed to make out a case against the accused men. He contended that the plot, if indeed there was one, was of such a whimsical and quixotic character that it was utterly impracticable and could never have been carried out. The facts of the case, according to Campbell, were simply that the emigrants, "enraged and disappointed at the detention of their vessel and the frustration of their expedition, through what he privately considered the officious interference of certain officials, had met together and talked wildly and at random about seizing the *Colon*." He pointed out that the defendents had no provisions, no cannon, and had not even provided themselves with a boat with which to board the Peruvian ship. The lawyer added that the idea was preposterous that the indicted men could board the steamer and take her out of the harbor against a headwind, past the guns of the *Shubrick*, Fort Point, Alcatraz, Black Point, and Angel Island, especially since the *Colon* had not taken on any coal. The judge of the case said he was inclined to agree that the conspiracy could not have been carried out successfully, but he thought that the matter should be investigated by a higher court. Therefore he held Williams, Colonel Daniel E. Hungerford, Lieutenant W. W. Bruce, John Ewald, William Burns, Louis de la Nord, James E. Clark, Sherman, John Thomas, and Titus Reynolds for trial at the county court on the charge of conspiracy to commit grand larceny and fixed their bail at $2,000 each.[31]

The second trial about a month later resuited in acquittal of the alleged pirates. It took the jury only a couple of minutes to bring in the verdict, according to a newspaper account of the proceedings. The *Daily Call*, in commenting on the end of the farce, lamented the expense incurred by the city in trying the guiltless men, and suggested that the San Francisco police were willing instruments of Napoleon's agents. The editor was more profound when he noted that "the object of the prime movers in the scheme, the French agents, has succeeded. They have accomplished their ends by breaking up the expedition which was about to sail to the aid of the Liberals in Mexico."[32]

In spite of months of planning, energetic and productive recruiting of volunteers, and the expenditure of over ten thousand dollars, the Arizona Exploring Expedition was a complete fiasco. During the two months of litigation and countermanding orders by various departments of the United States government most of the colonists became disillusioned and quit the expedition. In addition, Generals Vega and Williams were at odds owing to the piracy scandal. Vega did manage to salvage the arms and war stores that had been acquired for the campaign, and he later sent them to the Juárez forces in Mexico.[33]

After all the troubles with the *Brontes* group, Vega still hoped to send an armed corps to his native land. A year passed before plans materialized, but in July of 1866 another expedition got under way. This time Vega and the Californians had no difficulties with the customs or military authorities when they sailed from San Francisco aboard the bark *Keoka* and the brig *Josephine*. Many of the volunteers were "veterans" of the abortive exploring expedition: for example, Colonels Daniel E. Hungerford and Edward A. Lever, Captain Uladislao Vallejo, John Ewald, James Clark, and Juan Argos. There were about forty Americans and thirty Mexican officers on the voyage, and other men joined the expedition at Ensenada and La Paz, Baja, California. In addition to personnel the ships carried 7,000 rifles with caps, ball, and powder, and uniforms and other equipment for 3,000 soliders.[34]

Soon after debarkation at Dos Piedras near Topolobampo, Sinaloa, General Vega issued a proclamation announcing that at last he was able to return to his native land after fulfilling the confidential commission given him by the federal government. Dated August 15, 1866, the announcement was printed on a small press the agent had purchased in San Francisco, and he sent copies of the decree to some state and national officials. The broadside stated that Vega was accompanied by Mexican officers and soldiers as well as by "various foreigners who, after having heroically defended the cause of civilization and progress in the United States, now immigrate to our country." The manifesto also declared that Vega brought abundant top-quality war goods of the same quality currently used by the armies of the United States and England, and it invited all who were without arms to join his group "with the faith that it will be we who accompany Juárez in his triumphant return to the Palace of Montezuma."[35]

Vega's column then began a three-months' march over desert and mountains to Chihuahua, temporary capital of the republican government. Along the way ten of the Americans, including Colonel John B. Urmy and Lieutenant Colonel Albert Hahn, deserted Vega and took some of the munitions with them. The situation became even more serious when local civil and military authorities, who were not aware of Vega's secret commission or of his future plans, thought that the landing by the *Keoka* group might be an invasion of the state made for the purpose of overthrowing the interim government. There was even some speculation that the expeditionary force was destined to aid the imperial cause. Thus a military detachment under Colonel Adolfo Palacios was sent against Vega's foreign legion, but when the general presented his official orders from the supreme government, he and his corps were allowed to proceed toward Chihuahua.[36]

When Vega and his column reached the temporary capital of Chihuahua in mid-November of 1866, his troops were incorporated into the republican armed forces, but the general was accused of misappropriation of funds during his California residence. Not having his receipts and account books at hand, he could not render a full report at that time. A few months later General Vega published a booklet in which he itemized his California expenditures and receipts; with this public statement, copies of which he sent to various officials, he felt exonerated from the above-mentioned accusation. But the cabinet of the constitutional government wanted a detailed and personal report, and they ordered Vega to appear before them to present his account. Claiming that he was ill, Vega did not respond to the command performance request, whereupon the minister of war on May 2, 1867, issued an order to have him arrested as a deserter.[37]

---

[31] *Ibid.*, June 7, 1865.
[32] San Francisco *Daily Call*, July 16, 1865.
[33] Bancroft, 1888, **6**: p. 181, note 38.
[34] Men on the expedition listed in Plácido Vega Papers, **3**: fol. 438–439 and **4**: *comprobante* 9.
[35] Broadside in *ibid*. **3**: fol. 257.
[36] Buelna, 1924: p. 94. List of deserters in Plácido Vega Papers, **4**: *comprobante* 9, fol. 2.
[37] Copy of Vega's booklet in Plácido Vega Papers, **3**: fol. 708. Order for Vega's arrest in his military personnel file, *expediente* XI/111/3-1736, fol. 1, *hoja* 28, Archivo Histórico

By this time Vega had found refuge in the state of Tepic with his old friend Governor Manuel Lozada who had previously fallen out with Juárez. From Tepic, Vega and Lozada appealed to the republican officers at Querétaro to save Emperor Maximilian's life. Vega's letter, dated June 3, 1867, asked General Escobedo "to spare no effort using his powerful influence on the President to save Emperor Maximilian and his Generals from the death penalty." [38]

During the following decade Plácido Vega was involved in numerous revolts in the western and northern states of Mexico. In February, 1868, he was apprehended on Isla de Lobos, three miles off Mazatlán, but he escaped and returned to San Francisco, California, where he remained about a year. The following year he was filibustering in Sinaloa; later he joined uprisings known as Encarnación, Sufragio, and Tuxtepec. In the latter he cooperated with Porfirio Díaz in Nuevo León, and in 1876 he secured arms and military equipment from Texas to sustain the Díaz revolt. [39]

General Vega's colorful career ended on January 4, 1878, when he died in Acapulco apparently of natural causes. His death led to extensive litigation to determine his legal heir. Vega had at least two wives, Clara in Sinaloa and Sara in San Francisco, as well as a mistress, Anita Monsuy of Acapulco, and there were children by all of these unions. The matter was finally settled by the courts who found Plácido Vega y Vega, son of Clara, the legitimate heir and entitled to a pension from federal funds. [40]

Any appraisal of General Vega's career must include his accomplishments during the French intervention. After commanding troops in the front lines, Vega was entrusted with a top-secret commission to procure military supplies abroad. Working against difficult odds, he managed to send rifles and ammunition to Mexican field commanders and guerrilla chieftains who used them to liberate their regions from the French yoke. Some indication of his success as an arms runner is shown in Table I. As for human resources supplied by General Vega, it is difficult to evaluate their military contribution to the victory of the liberal forces. Vega's volunteers were few in numbers, but these well-trained soldiers from the United States, fighting alongside the Juaristas, provided a symbolic and psychological stimulus to the struggle. Some of the Yankee volunteers were recruited by General Vega; others by an associate of his, General Gasper Sánchez Ochoa, whose career as a secret agent will be traced in the chapter that follows.

V. GENERAL SÁNCHEZ OCHOA—INTRIGUES WITH FRÉMONT

Only one of the Mexican secret agents in the United States during the 1860's operated on both the Pacific and Atlantic coasts. This peripatetic commissioner, General Gaspar Sánchez Ochoa, was a war hero who had been wounded in battle on three occasions, and no doubt it was his military prowess and distinguished record that shielded him from the postwar ignominy suffered by his companions in arms and fellow agents, Plácido Vega and José Carvajal.[1]

Sánchez Ochoa, who was born in Guadalajara on January 6, 1837, was educated at the mining college in Mexico City. He entered the army as a lieutenant of engineers in 1855, and for the next fifty-three years his career was linked with that branch of the Mexican military establishment. In the War of the Reform he fought with the liberal forces, and during the French intervention he took part in the 1863 defense of Puebla. When that city fell to the French forces, Colonel Sánchez Ochoa and his commanding officer, General González Ortega, were taken as prisoners of war, but both managed to escape and make their way to the Juárez headquarters in San Luis Potosí.[2]

Colonel Sánchez Ochoa was subsequently ordered to Mazatlán to erect fortifications in that port. At the end of March, 1864, the French warship *Cordelière* tried to land troops and occupy the city, but the Mexican colonel, almost singlehandedly, repelled the French attack. On this occasion he demonstrated such bravery that he was congratulated by the captain of the English ship *Caribdis* who witnessed the entire military operation. The accomplishment later earned Sánchez Ochoa a promotion to the rank of general and appointment as military commandant and governor of Sinaloa.[3]

Advice from several United States citizens residing in Mazatlán led General Sánchez Ochoa to believe that Mexican bonds secured by customhouse receipts could be sold in San Francisco, California. He passed this information on to the Juárez cabinet, and on December 31, 1864, they authorized him to negotiate a foreign loan, the proceeds to be used for purchase of war vessels and munitions. The Mexican general then asked his government for an increase in the amount of the projected loan and for a more detailed set of orders with the various powers listed separately.[4] Subsequently, the foreign minister sent him six dispatches dated March 1,

---

Militar, Secretaría de Defensa Nacional, Mexico, hereafter cited as ADN.

[38] Plácido Vega Papers, 3: fol. 317–318; for Escobedo's reply and related correspondence, see *ibid.* 3: fol. 319–328.

[39] *Expediente* XI/111/3-1736, fol. 1, *hojas* 34–49, 75, ADN. Vega's defection and later life in Cosío Villegas, 1955–1965: 1: pp. 537–539, 857–858; see also *expediente* XI/111/3-1737, fol. 1, *hoja* 75, ADN; Buelna, 1884, p. 22; Frias y Soto, 1905: p. 352.

[40] *Expediente* XI/111/3-1736, fol. 1, *hojas* 75, 90, ADN; Sara Vega to Platón Vallejo, San Francisco, August 29, 1890, Mariano G. Vallejo Papers, Sonoma State Historical Park, Sonoma, California; Anita Monsuy to Vega, Acapulco, January 9, 1864, Plácido Vega Papers, 3: fol. 767–770.

[1] Sánchez Lamego, 1952: pp. 180–181.
[2] *Ibid.*, p. 178; see also Godoy, 1898: p. 272.
[3] Sánchez Lamego, 1952: pp. 181–182; Buelna, 1884: pp. 28–30.
[4] Sánchez Ochoa to Lerdo de Tejada, February 6, 1865, in Mexico, Legación, *Contratos*, 1868: pp. 269–271.

1865, which together constitute his instructions and authority.[5]

The Juárez cabinet empowered General Sánchez Ochoa to travel to San Francisco, California, where he could issue $10,000,000 in bonds bearing six per cent interest "more or less" and secured by the mining taxes and customhouse revenues of Sonora and Sinaloa. With income derived from the sale of the bonds the general was authorized to purchase up to six ships, he having the right to command them or name their captains. Acquisition of 60,000 rifles and a "proportionate amount" of artillery, cavalry arms, and munitions was also authorized as was the recruitment of foreigners for service in the Mexican army. By his written orders Sánchez Ochoa could organize the foreign volunteers and name their officers.[6]

In accordance with the broad powers enumerated above, the Juarist agent proceeded to San Francisco where he arrived early in May, 1865. He was accompanied by his chief of staff, Colonel George M. Green, formerly of San Francisco. Also on the voyage from La Paz, Baja California, was Green's brother, Alfred A. Green, a former member of the California legislature who was at that time engaged in agricultural and mining pursuits in Sinaloa. Frederick G. Fitch, an American mining engineer, was a member of the Sánchez Ochoa coterie, but he took an earlier ship from Mazatlán arriving in California in April, 1865. Fitch and Alfred Green were promised $50,000 each by the Mexican general for their anticipated services on behalf of the Mexican republic, as were two other men, Richard Chenery and Edward Slosson. Sánchez Ochoa signed a contract with the latter two authorizing them to purchase the ships and arms specified in the general's commission.[7]

Sánchez Ochoa's arrival in San Francisco coincided with General Plácido Vega's attempt to send 400 armed men to Mexico, but the two commissioners could not agree on plans or work together for the common goal of the restoration of the republic. Although Vega had recently received permission from Juárez to float a loan in California, he proposed that only one Mexican loan should be negotiated and asked Sánchez Ochoa for $125,000 from the ten-million-dollar proposed bond issue. The latter's reply was that he had neither the funds nor authority from the government to aid another secret agent.[8]

Another point of conflict was the recruitment of men for military service in Mexico; the two secret agents

FIG. 3. General Gaspar Sánchez Ochoa, Mexican secret agent in California and New York. Photo courtesy of the California Historical Society.

vied with each other in trying to enlist the same soldiers of fortune. When Vega's plans for the *Brontes* expedition failed in May, 1865, Sánchez Ochoa enticed a group of Vega's men to his camp and arranged to send them to Mexico under his chief of staff, Colonel George Green. Some credit for this effort belongs to San Francisco capitalist Samuel Brannan who paid the costs of outfitting the volunteers known as the Brannan Contingent of the Mexican Republican Army. As will be seen in the following chapter, this group joined the American Legion of Honor and fought in Mexico.

Meanwhile, Sánchez Ochoa and his assistants proceeded to negotiate contracts for arms and to initiate propaganda activities on behalf of the Mexican republic. The Green brothers and their nephew Francis L. Green, along with Frederick G. Fitch, organized and directed the Monroe League of California. This group was formed to secure moral and material aid for Mexico, and at the meetings in various California cities speakers called on Americans to support the Monroe Doctrine.[9] The activites of this organization paralleled the Mexican

---

[5] Details on Sánchez Ochoa's bond issue in Frazer, 1942: pp. 397–414.

[6] Complete instructions in Mexico, Legación, *Contratos*, 1868: pp. 265–275.

[7] Green, 1870: pp. 8–9, Fitch, 1870: p. 5. Contracts with Chenery and Slossen in Mexico, Legación, *Contratos*, 1868: pp. 351–352.

[8] Vega to Sánchez Ochoa, and Sánchez Ochoa to Vega, June 21, 1865, Plácido Vega Papers, 2: fol. 417–422.

[9] Fitch, 1870: pp. 5–6; advertisement of meeting in *Alta California*, July 10, 1865.

Fig. 4. $1,000 Mexican Bond issued by General Sánchez Ochoa. Reproduction courtesy of Bancroft Library

Clubs formed by General Vega, but the latter groups were formed around the Spanish-speaking population of California while the Monroe League meetings were generally conducted in English.

The principal reason for General Sánchez Ochoa's mission to California was to float a loan, and through his American friends and assistants he was introduced to the San Francisco banker, Samuel Brannan, who promised to aid with the bond issue. Brannan provided $30,000 in gold coin to pay for the costs of preparing the bonds and for other expenses of the Mexican agent. For this consideration the banker was named as agent for the sale of the bonds with a commission of one per cent on all sales. To secure payment of the bonds and interest coupons attached thereto, one-half of the revenue from the customhouses of Manzanillo, Mazatlán, and Guaymas was assigned and conveyed to Sam Brannan.[10]

The Mexican bond offering was advertised in San Francisco newspapers where it was noted that bonds were available in denominations from $50 to $1,000. The securities were to be sold at fifty cents on the dollar and they would mature in six years. Interest was ten per cent per year with payment to be made semi-annually in gold coin at the Pacific Bank in San Francisco.[11]

In spite of high interest and an attractive discount the Mexican bonds did not sell. Of course Mexico's credit rating was directly related to its domestic posture, and in the summer of 1865 President Juárez had his back to the wall having withdrawn steadily northward until he was at Paso del Norte on the Rio Grande. Under the circumstances California investors were hesitant to speculate in securities issued by a government that might not be in existence when the bonds matured. And even though the obligation was secured by the custom revenues from Mexican Pacific coast ports, the fact was that these very same harbors were actually under the control and flag of the French imperialists.

When the bond issue failed, the Mexican commissioner was obliged to make a new agreement with his banker. By the terms of three covenants signed on September 26, 1865, in lieu of the agent's commission and in consideration of money advanced, Sánchez Ochoa agreed to pay Brannan $30,000 in gold within sixty days with interest at one and a half per cent per month until paid. However, if payment were made in legal tender notes rather than gold, the principal would be $43,478.26 with the cited interest rate. To guarantee payment the Mexican general hypothecated the entire ten million dollars in bonds to the San Franciscan.[12]

Backers of the bond issue then convinced Sánchez Ochoa that he should go to the American financial capital and introduce the bonds in the New York market. In the latter part of October, 1865, he and his associates Fitch, Chenerey, and Green took the ten million dollars in bonds and moved across the country to the Atlantic coast. Chenery had a power of attorney authorizing him to dispose of the bonds subject to the Mexican general's approval, and Alfred A. Green had a special interest in the bonds since he had contracted with Brannan to split the one per cent commission, with Green to receive three-eighths and the banker five-eighths of the amount.[13]

The arrival in New York of General Sánchez Ochoa and his aides was inopportune since another Mexican commissioner, General José M. Carvajal, was in that city and had made arrangements to float $30,000,000 in bonds of the Mexican republic. The Mexican minister to the United States saw that marketing both issues bearing different interest and discount rates would cause confusion and undermine the success of the venture, but by promising a portion of the revenue from the larger loan to Sánchez Ochoa the latter agreed to withhold his bonds from the market.[14] It should also be noted that Carvajal had agreed with the firm handling his securities that no other Mexican bonds would be issued while his were being negotiated.

When the Mexican government heard that Sánchez Ochoa had gone to New York to float a loan, the foreign minister informed the general that he would have to secure the prior approval of Romero for all future contracts. Later when the foreign minister learned that the commissioner had pledged the bonds to Sam Brannan, he wrote Romero that Sánchez Ochoa's mission

---

[10] Sánchez Ochoa-Brannan contract and power of attorney in U.S. Congress, *House Exec. Doc. 33*, pp. 199–202.
[11] San Francisco *Daily Call*, July 4–11, 1865, advertisement, p. 3.
[12] September agreements in U.S. Congress, *House Exec. Doc. 33*, pp. 225–226.
[13] Mexico, Legación, *Contratos*, 1868: pp. 349–351, 360.
[14] Mexico, Legación, *Circulares*, 1868: 1: p. 360.

was "to procure a loan and not to impede one by issuing bonds for millions and then pledging all of them for a small sum of ready cash."[15] In order to coordinate the bond and loan negotiations, the Mexican minister requested copies of all the documents that Sánchez Ochoa had signed in San Francisco. Instead of papers the general sent his adjutant, Frederick Fitch, who read some of the contracts to Romero but did not supply transcripts of them.[16] In spite of repeated requests for copies of the documents, the Mexican commissioner ignored Romero and continued to act without consulting the minister.

Both Sánchez Ochoa and Carvajal tried to promote a legislative resolution by the United States Congress whereby this country would guarantee payment of the Mexican bonds in case of default by the neighboring republic. Such a pledge would assure a successful sale which in turn would give a great advantage to the Juárez administration. It would also mean that the commissioners would have a considerable amount of funds at their disposal, and it would be an achievement in line with their instructions. Carvajal hired a propaganda agent to influence the congressional vote, while Sánchez Ochoa's aides, Green and Fitch, published a weekly pamphlet, *The Vindication of Liberal Mexico,* copies of which were sent to the president and members of Congress in Washington.[17]

But it was the soldier-explorer-politician, General John Charles Frémont, that Sánchez Ochoa saw as the redeemer of republican Mexico. With his experience, contacts, and personal prestige surely he could railroad through Congress a guarantee of Mexican bonds. Frémont was sympathetic to the cause of liberal, republican Mexico; so moved was he that he agreed to help with the attempt to influence Congress for only a few concessions—six million of the ten million dollars of Sánchez Ochoa bonds and a grant to build a railroad across northern Mexico.

After resigning his army commission in 1864, Frémont became interested in western railroad projects, and it was the prospect of a railroad concession in Mexico that drew him to Sánchez Ochoa. In the early part of 1866 Frémont acquired a large block of stock in the Memphis and El Paso Railroad which, although it had no track or locomotives, was chartered and had generous land grants in the Southwest.[18] A great system operating to California with connections from Texas to the Pacific ports of Mexico was visualized by the promoter as he entered into various agreements with the Mexican commissioner.

On February 2, 1866, Frémont and Sánchez Ochoa signed a contract by which the latter as an agent of the Mexican republic conceded to the former the right to build a railroad from Guaymas, a port on the Gulf of California, to some point of contact with the projected Texas-California railroad. According to the covenant the Mexican government was also obliged to grant terms similar to those given by the United States to the builders of transcontinental railroads—large land grants, financial aid for the construction and maintenance of the roadbed, exemption from duties and taxes, as well as free transit for goods and passengers during construction. In return for this generous grant Frémont agreed to further the cause of the Mexican republic through public meetings, the press, and by using means he thought convenient. It was clearly stated that Frémont would try to improve the commercial value of the Mexican bonds, and to realize this end Sánchez Ochoa promised to give him six million of the ten million dollars in bonds which had been printed in San Francisco.[19] Nothing was said about the fact that the Mexican general had already pledged the total bond issue to Sam Brannan to guarantee his advance of thirty thousand dollars.

Romero was astonished when he was given a copy of the agreement, and he immediately notified the Mexican government about the arrangements concluded by General Sánchez Ochoa. The minister of foreign relations had been so disgusted over previous contracts negotiated by the secret agent that he declared his commission at an end and ordered him to return to Mexico. However, the general was authorized to remain in the United States to assist in settling pending affairs so long as Romero consented to this arrangement. Then when the foreign minister heard about the Sánchez Ochoa-Frémont contract, he declared all the commissioner's acts to be null and void. In a dispatch to Romero he pointed out that Sánchez Ochoa had exceeded his authorization by giving railroad concessions, by pledging bonds to Frémont, and by failing to secure prior approval of his acts from the Mexican minister.[20]

Soon after Romero informed Sánchez Ochoa that his commission had been revoked by the Mexican government, the secret commissioner and his friend Frémont began to gravitate to the schismatic political faction of General Jesús González Ortega. The latter was president of the supreme court of Mexico, and the constitution of that country called for the holder of that office to succeed to the presidency on the vacancy of the highest office. President Juárez's elected term of office expired in 1865, but because of the French intervention and the impossibility of holding a national election, Juárez declared that he would continue in office for the

---

[15] Lerdo de Tejada to Romero, Paso del Norte, January 16, 1866, in Mexico, Legación, *Contratos,* 1868: p. 291.

[16] Frazer, 1942: p. 400.

[17] Fitch, 1870: p. 6; Mexico, Legación, *Contratos,* 1868: p. 356.

[18] Goodwin, 1930: pp. 240–242.

[19] A final copy of the contract signed by the principals and approved by General González Oretga, "Interim Constitutional President of Mexico," in Jesús González Ortega Papers, Bancroft Library.

[20] Lerdo de Tejada to Romero, Paso del Norte, January 16 and April 11, 1866, in Mexico, Legación, *Contratos,* 1868; pp. 283–284, 292–293.

duration of the emergency. González Ortega claimed the decree was unconstitutional, and he publicly protested, calling on other Mexicans to support his position.[21]

General González Ortega was living in New York City when he announced his claim as interim constitutional president of Mexico, whereupon supporters of Juárez replied that the general was out of the country without permission and thereby not in a position to rule on the legality of executive decrees. Furthermore, they said that Juárez was not only holding onto his post, but he was holding together the remnants of the Mexican republic while González Ortega had abandoned the front line of defense by going into exile. In any event, Sánchez Ochoa and Frémont went over to the side of the presidential pretender, and they got him to approve their contract for the railroad to Guaymas.[22]

Although González Ortega did not receive a commission to go abroad in order to raise men and resources for the Mexican defense effort, a volunteer force of over 100,000 American war veterans was organized by Colonel William H. Allen who claimed to be an agent of the Mexican general.[23] This large-scale recruitment effort resembled other similar movements in that the men were supposed to go to Mexico as armed colonists rather than soldiers. Colonel Allen, late of the 1st and 145th New York Volunteers, founded the Mexican Emigration Company in May, 1865, with offices in New York, Washington, Baltimore, Philadelphia, and other cities. In addition to notices of company meetings, Allen inserted advertisements in metropolitan newspapers reading as follows:

MEXICO, MAXIMILIAN AND MONROE DOCTRINE. All persons who desire joining a company soon starting "to make a strike" for fame and fortune in the land of golden ores and luscious fruits, aided and protected by the patriotic President of that republic, will please address Benito J. Juarez, box 5,614 New York post office.[24]

A call was sent out by the Mexican Emigration Company for interested persons to register their names and former military ranks at one of three centers in New York: 144 Second Street, 35 Third Avenue, or the corner of Howard and Crosby Streets. The New York *Herald* reported that on May 10, 1865, no less than 435 men signed their names on company rolls.[25] The enthusiasm is in part explained by the fact that the American Civil War was in the final stage, and military groups were being rapidly demobilized. In addition to those that came in person, a number of veterans applied by mail for service with the projected corps. There are almost one hundred letters addressed to Colonel Allen, General González Ortega, or the general's secretary, Colonel Juan Togño, in the collection of González Ortega Papers in the Bancroft Library at the University of California. Most of the applicants were former officers in the Union army, and they desired to raise and lead a company or a brigade of their former comrades.

For the nationwide organization of the projected military colonization movement Colonel Allen called on his acquaintances in the United States Army and the Confederate States Army. By June 20, 1865, he had reports from thirty-four officers who had enrolled a grand total of 109,000 men for service in Mexico. The ease with which such a tremendous number of men could be enlisted for Mexican service gives some idea of the interest in that country's plight at the end of the Civil War. It also reflects the lack of opportunity at home for the returning veterans as well as the spirit of adventure born in a long domestic war. The list in table 2 shows commanding officers, their geographical station, and the number of men they enrolled. Although this muster roll was no doubt padded, even ten or twenty per cent of the total would have been a formidable expeditionary force. Colonel Allen submitted this report to General González Ortega along with a letter written in his colorful and colloquial hand in which he noted that the officers were:

Engageing in The Present Movement not for Wealth alone —but fame, and To assist in Carring Out a Principle Long Established in the American Mind—That of Non Intervention By European Powers in State affairs on This Continent . . . Such Body of Men have Ever Been Organized and heald Togeather at So Slight an Expense as that now Controaled by Me.[26]

But this vast paper army was never given its marching orders. Owing to a limited supply of funds, Colonel Allen could not keep the men waiting indefinitely and, when financial assistance was not forthcoming from González Ortega, the organization disintegrated as rapidly as it was formed. The men were willing enough to fight in Mexico, but only as long as they received their pay and enlistment bonuses.

The relationship between Colonel Allen and González Ortega was indeed a strange one, for the general would not allow his name to be used by the colonel, nor did he apparently ever reply to Allen's many letters and petitions. In the end, which came in October, 1865, when Allen sued to recover some of his expenditures, González Ortega denied that he had ever encouraged Allen in any way, nor had he promised him any money or reimbursements, and he swore that he had requested the colonel to desist from writing to him. González

---

[21] Owen, 1866: No. 5. González Ortega's correspondence with General Vega, in which the latter supported Juárez, is in Plácido Vega Papers, 3: fol. 105–125, 196–212. The legal question is examined in a book by the pretender's grandson, González Ortega, 1941. See also Cadenhead, 1972.

[22] Decree of González Ortega, New York, February 22, 1866, authorizing Frémont and others to build a railroad to Guaymas, Mexico, in Jesús González Ortega Papers.

[23] Allen to González Ortega, New York, June 20, 1865, *ibid.*

[24] New York *Herald*, May 5, 6, 7, 1865; see also Washington *Chronicle*, May 5, 1865.

[25] New York *Herald*, May 11, 1865: p. 5.

[26] Allen to González Ortega [New York] June 30, 1865, Jesús González Ortega Papers.

TABLE 2

American Officers and Men Enrolled for Service in Mexico; Col. Allen's Report to Gen. González Ortega, June 20, 1865

[Original roster, González Ortega Papers, Bancroft Library]

Station	Commanding Officer	Number of Men
St. Louis, Mo.	Brig. Gen. R. C. Howard	8,000
Louisville, Ky.	Lt. Col. H. A. Wilson	3,000
Memphis, Tenn.	Col. Edward Clark	5,000
Central Ky.	Brevet Maj. Wm. Confort	3,000
Cincinnati, Ohio	Col. Herman T. Kooff	3,800
Columbus, Ohio	Col. E. Whistler	3,400
Cleveland, Ohio	Brev. Brig. Gen. Kirtland	3,000
Sandusky, Ohio	Lt. Col. Wilson	1,800
Chicago, Illinois	Maj. J. M. Lye	4,000
Detroit, Mich.	Capt. E. Booking	3,500
St. Paul, Minn.	Brig. Gen. Swift	6,000
Ft. Leavenworth [Kan.]	Col. Wilson	3,000
Buffalo, N. Y.	Col. McNally	4,000
Rochester, N. Y.	Col. Parker	1,600
Utica, N. Y.	Maj. Kemp	1,500
Albany, N. Y.	Capt. Bailey	3,000
Boston, Mass.	Brig. Gen. R. C. Cowden	5,000
Manchester, N. H.	Capt. D. C. Wells	3,700
Hallowall, Maine	Capt. Gilman	4,000
Providence, R. I.	Lt. Col. Post	1,200
Hartford, Conn.	Capt. Kraszorski	1,800
Philadelphia, Pa.	Maj. Otto Swartz	1,100
Wilmington, Del.	Capt. Wimberley	400
Baltimore, Md.	Lt. Col. Thos. Clowdsley	2,300
Washington, D. C.	Capt. Samuel Edwards	1,100
Camp Stonemen, D. C.	Capt. Deigman	400
Alexandria, Va.	Maj. J. F. Thomas	1,700
Richmond, Va.	Col. Spafford (CSA)	7,000
Wilmington, N. C.	Lt. Col. Jamieson (CSA)	3,700
Savannah, Ga.	Col. McTash (CSA)	3,700
Mobile, Ala.	Maj. John Young	2,000
New Orleans, La.	Lt. Col. Young (CSA)	No report
Jacksonville, Fla.	Lt. Snyder	No report
New York City	[Col. Wm. H. Allen]	14,000
	Total	109,000

Ortega also averred that he had destroyed all the letters written to him by Allen, and he said that he had never received a report of the men enrolled by Allen.[27] However, the report of June 20 cited above and ten letters from Allen to the general were among the latter's papers which were taken from him when he was detained by United States military authorities while returning to Mexico in November, 1866.

After the affair with Colonel Allen, González Ortega made his claim to the presidency of Mexico, and subsequently he became involved in the projects of Sánchez Ochoa and Frémont. In February of 1866 he approved the contract whereby Frémont was to build a railroad to Guaymas, Mexico. During March, April, and May, Frémont was soliciting both factions for concessions; his projected compacts with Romero, who represented Juárez, were all rejected because he refused to renounce the railroad grant made by the now discredited Sánchez Ochoa.[28] From May to November, 1866, Frémont and Sánchez Ochoa pinned their hopes on the success of González Ortega's pretension of executive authority, and they proposed several important contracts which they anticipated would be approved by the interim constitutional president of Mexico.

An unpublished draft agreement between Sánchez Ochoa and Frémont, dated May, 1866, called for the latter's assistance in promoting the sale of $50,000,000 in Mexican bonds for which he would receive a commission of two per cent on the sales. There was also envisaged the organization of five American volunteer brigades of 3,000 men each who would fight under the Mexican flag. Frémont was to name all the officers of these units, and of course he and Sánchez Ochoa would have their choice of commands. This eleven-page document contains an interesting plan of future opera-

---

[27] Transcript of testimony in Allen versus González Ortega, October 14, 1865, *ibid.*

[28] Romero-Frémont parley in Frazer, 1942: pp. 404–409.

tions by which the Mexican cities would be retaken, beginning with Matamoros and working south toward Durango, San Luis Potosí, Querétaro, and Mexico City. There was also to be a naval squadron of eleven ships fitted out in Boston and New York with Sánchez Ochoa in command of this Mexican armada aboard his "monitor," the *Monroe Doctrine*. In the land operations Frémont would lead two divisions of 12,000 men in the army of liberation, and Sánchez Ochoa was scheduled to be the commander-in-chief of the army that would triumphantly enter Mexico City.[29]

In September, 1866, the same parties proposed two more contracts, one of which authorized Frémont to build an interoceanic canal across Mexico, and the other gave him a thirty-year concession to establish banks of issue in Mazatlán and Matamoros.[30] A draft of the latter contract indicates that Sánchez Ochoa became an agent of González Ortega once he had lost his commission from the Juárez government.

Although González Ortega and five other Mexican officers returned to Mexico late in 1866, Sánchez Ochoa remained in the United States for another six months. In addition to having his special commissioner status revoked by the Juárez government he suffered another loss of power and prestige when his army commission was suspended because he failed to report for new orders as commanded.[31] Early in 1867 it became apparent to Sánchez Ochoa that González Ortega was not going to become president of Mexico. Indeed, when the presidential pretender returned to his fatherland, he could not enlist the support of even a dozen Mexicans, and he was imprisoned by the governor of Zacatecas in accordance with decrees of the national government.[32]

With the failure of the González Ortega movement and the downgrading of Sánchez Ochoa the latter's aides became disillusioned with their chief, and they parted from him. They had long since lost all hope of ever receiving the $50,000 promised each of them. Alfred A. Green later petitioned Romero for reimbursement for services rendered the Mexican republic, and the minister gave him $500 to estop all future claims against Sánchez Ochoa or the government of Mexico. However, Green and Fitch later submitted appeals for their $50,000 plus interest to the United States–Mexican Claims Commission of 1868–1876.[33] Their petitions were denied.

The final act of Sánchez Ochoa's sojourn in the United States was a dramatic confession and request for absolution. In March of 1867 he visited the Mexican legation in Washington where, in a series of interviews with the secretary and Minister Romero, he acknowledged his past errors and asked for amnesty and assistance in rehabilitation. The ex-agent recanted the heresy of having supported González Ortega in his bid for the presidency of Mexico, and he repented his indiscretion for having united with Frémont. He related what he knew about the status of his bonds, and he gave additional information about some of the contracts he had signed with Frémont and other speculators. He also informed the legation that Frémont had given him several hundred dollars and promised him several hundred thousand dollars for concessions granted. After declaring his intention of returning home Sánchez Ochoa asked the minister to forward a personal letter to Juárez in which he asked for reinstatement in the Mexican army.[34]

Finally, early in June of 1867 Sánchez Ochoa left New York for New Orleans and Mexico after having his hotel bills paid by the Mexican minister who also advanced him money for transportation. In justifying this expense to the foreign minister, Romero wrote that it was better to spend a few hundred dollars in this way than to permit the ex-general to remain abroad making agreements that would cost the Mexican government much more in the end.[35] Sánchez Ochoa entered Mexico under the name of Pablo Aguirre, but when he arrived in San Luis Potosí, he was recognized, apprehended, and jailed. In August he escaped and made his way to Zacatecas where, suffering from hunger and lack of resources and friends, he turned himself in to the authorities. Charged with having conspired against the constitutional government of Mexico, he was sent to a military prison in Mexico City.[36]

The rehabilitation of Sánchez Ochoa was comparatively quick and easy. Less than two years after his inglorious and incognito return to Mexico he appeared as one of the official hosts who entertained the former secretary of state, William H. Seward, and his party of Americans on their visit to Mexico in 1869–1870. One member of the group recorded the fact that General Sánchez Ochoa owned the vast estate on which the volcano Popocatépetl was situated; it appears that the general's financial status had indeed improved since his return to Mexico. In December, 1871, he was reinstated as a general of engineers in the Mexican army, and he later served for eighteen years as chief of engineers in the war department. Subsequently he was a judge on the military supreme court, holding that post until 1907 when he retired. General Gasper Sánchez Ochoa died in Mexico City on September 18, 1908.[37]

---

[29] Draft of the May, 1866, contract in Jesús González Ortega Papers.
[30] Copies of the contracts in *ibid*.
[31] Sánchez Lamego, 1952: pp. 182–183.
[32] González Ortega, 1941: pp. 368–369.
[33] Green claimed $330,938 and Fitch $217,300, U.S. Congress, *Senate Exec. Doc. 31*, pp. 54–55; see also Mexico, Legación, *Contratos*, 1868: pp. 420–428.

[34] Memo of Ignacio Mariscal, Washington, March 11, 1867, in Mexico, Legación, *Contratos*, 1868: pp. 391–394.
[35] Juan N. Navarro to Romero, New York, June 8, 1867, and Romero to Lerdo de Tejada, May 16, 1867, *ibid*., pp. 408–410.
[36] Sánchez Lamego, 1952: p. 183.
[37] Evans, 1879: p. 264; Sánchez Lamego, 1952: pp. 183–184.

As for the place of the Sánchez Ochoa mission to the United States in the history of the French intervention, it must be concluded that this assignment was almost totally fruitless. Although sent abroad to procure a loan of several million dollars he did not raise even a *centavo* for his government. Without funds he could not carry out other provisions of his commission, the forwarding of ships and arms to Mexico. Not only was his mission unproductive, it had a negative effect on the efforts of the Juárez government when he joined the sectarian González Ortega faction and when he began to grant concessions that were not in the national interest. But the rapid redemption of the secret agent from failure and near-treason indicates that the Juárez government was ready to forgive those republicans who repented their misdeeds, especially since there were so many inexpiable sinners in Mexico—those who had collaborated with the French during the intervention. One positive achievement of Sánchez Ochoa's mission was the contingent of volunteers he recruited in San Francisco who joined the American Legion of Honor and fought in Mexico. The story of that military corps follows.

VI. THE AMERICAN LEGION OF HONOR IN MEXICO

The American Legion of Honor was an elite company of former United States soldiers who went in various contingents to Mexico where their officers were commissioned by President Juárez. This corps fought in several battles preceding the downfall of the empire, and Legion officers were present at the surrender and execution of Maximilian as well as the triumphal entry of Juárez into Mexico City in the summer of 1867. Although there were more than one hundred officers in the American Legion of Honor, its existence has been generally ignored by historians on both sides of the Rio Grande.[1]

The most reliable and extensive information about the Legion of Honor can be found in sworn testimony of some thirty-five Legionnaires before the United States–Mexican Claims Commission of 1868. This international board was formed to settle outstanding claims of citizens of both nations; claimants who were members the Legion protested that they had not received their full pay and bonuses as promised by the Juárez government. Statements of the men, now deposited in Washington in the National Archives, are accompanied by many supporting documents including original Mexican army commissions signed by President Juárez.[2] The Claims Commission awarded payments to only a few of the men because most of them had signed a waiver of

FIG. 5. Colonel George M. Green, commander of the American Legion of Honor in Mexico. Photo courtesy of the California Historical Society.

future claims at the time of their discharge from the Mexican army.

Yankee soldiers of fortune were drawn to Mexico in the 1860's for various reasons, but one important stimulus was financial remuneration. Base pay for foreigners who joined the republican army was comparable to that of the United States military forces. In addition there were monetary prizes for bravery and outstanding service as well as a land grant to all soldiers. Mexican citizenship was also granted to foreign volunteers.[3] Given the attractive pay and bonus schedule and considering the great number of unemployed veterans in the United States following the long domestic war, is it any wonder that so many men went to Mexico?

Propaganda stressing French violation of the Monroe Doctrine was also effective in gaining recruits for the Mexican front. Groups organized in the United States to aid the republic of Mexico held fund-raising banquets, torchlight parades, and mass meetings. In the Mid-West, General Lew Wallace of Indiana, founder of the Mexican Aid Society, hoped that his organization and its affiliates would "control public sentiment, govern the politicians, raise funds, recruit soldiers, and beget cooperation and united intelligent management."[4] On the East Coast, Ephraim G. Squier, a former diplomat who had represented the United States in Latin America, headed the Monroe Doctrine Committee. Squier ex-

---

[1] The only two articles about the Legion were published ninety years apart; see Cornwall, 1871, and Miller, 1961.

[2] Commissions in Harvey Lake versus Mexico, U.S. National Archives, Record Group 76, United States–Mexican Claims Commission, 1868–1876, docket 607, cited hereafter as NA/RG 76 followed by doc. no. See also NA/RG 76, docs. 906, 908.

[3] For pay and bonuses see chapter II, note 34.

[4] Wallace to Thomas Buchanan Read, April 30, 1865, Lew Wallace Collection, Indiana Historical Society.

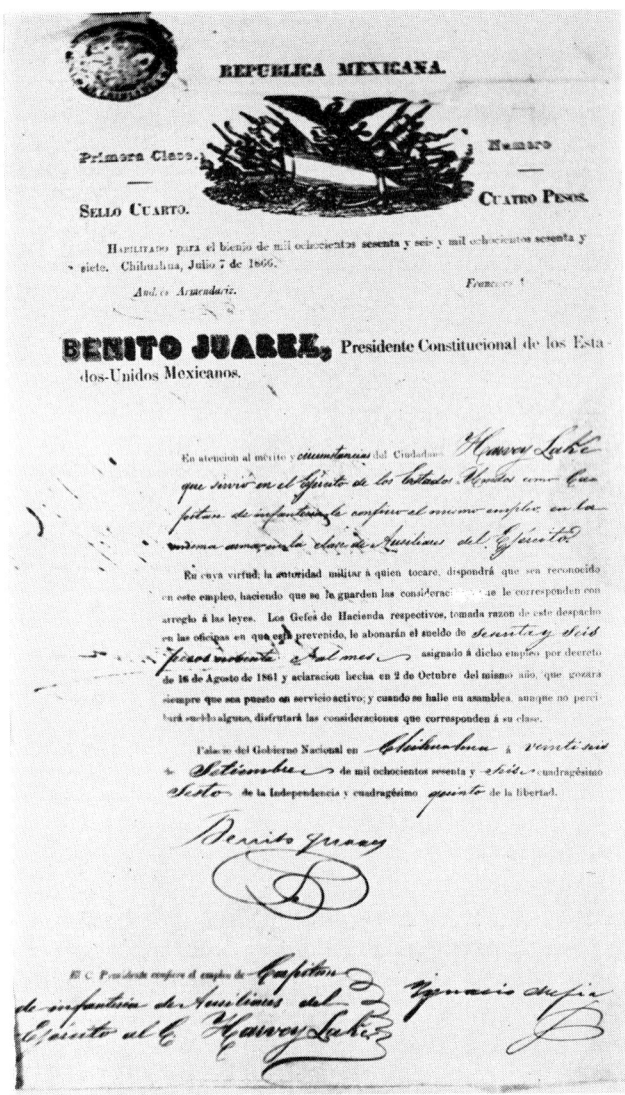

FIG. 6. Mexican army commission of Captain Harvey Lake, American Legion of Honor. Reproduction courtesy of the U.S. National Archives.

pressed poetically the sentiments of his group, "If the old-world minions on our continent remain, we'll take the old familiar guns, and go with Grant again."[5] Meanwhile, in California, Generals Vega and Sánchez Ochoa had organized Mexican Clubs and Monroe Doctrine Leagues with similar goals.

Although some later contingents came from other parts of the country, the American Legion of Honor had its origin in San Francisco, California. Two nucleus groups of armed soldiers were recruited in that city by Mexican secret agents, Generals Plácido Vega and Gaspar Sánchez Ochoa. The latter's chief of staff, Colonel George M. Green, screened the initial men, all Union veterans, for the Legion and accompanied them to Mexico.

Colonel George Mason Green was an excellent choice as first commander of the American Legion of Honor. Completely bilingual and an officer in the Mexican army for the previous eight years, he quickly won the respect of his Yankee followers. Born in New Brunswick in 1836, he had emigrated to California in 1852 then spent some time in Mexico as an itinerant photographer before joining the Mexican army in 1858.[6] He had six brothers who were active in politics and business in California and Mexico. One brother, Alfred A. Green, was a former California legislator who served as a financial and propaganda agent for General Sánchez Ochoa and assisted him in floating a $10,000,000 bond issue in San Francisco in 1865. Another member of the family, Francis L. Green, joined the Legion and fought in the battles of Zacatecas, Querétaro, and the siege of Mexico City.[7]

Second in command of the Legion was Captain Harvey Lake, an officer in the California militia and a former infantry captain in the United States Army. Lake was teaching military tactics at the San Francisco armory when he joined Colonel Green and the defenders of the Mexican republic. These two officers secured arms and equipment for their original force from Sam Brannan, a San Francisco banker who sympathized with the cause of Juárez. Brannan furnished the original contingent of twenty-seven men with complete uniforms, thirty-five saddle horses, sabres, Henry repeating rifles, Colt pistols, 16,500 rounds of ammunition, two wagons, and a supply of drugs and medical equipment.[8]

In June of 1866, Colonel Green received orders to mobilize his men and join Juárez on the Mexican–United States border at Paso del Norte. The Legion of Honor made the trip to Juárez's headquarters in ninety days, traveling by sea to Southern California then by horseback to Chihuahua. They departed from San Francisco on June 15, 1866, aboard the steamship *Pacific*, and one of the soldiers noted, "We had to embark on the sly under pretence of being miners bound for Arizona, to avoid the interference of enemies of the Mexican Republic."[9] From San Pedro, California, the armed company proceeded to Texas by way of Fort Yuma, Arizona Territory, then across New Mexico Territory. In August when they reached Paso del Norte on the Rio Grande, they discovered that President

---

[5] Squier to Maj. Gen. N. P. Banks, December 28, 1865, in Harrington, 1948: p. 193.

[6] George M. Green, manuscript account, "Statement of his Recollections of Life in Mexico, 1853 to 1855," Bancroft Library.

[7] Daniel Green versus Mexico, NA/RG 76, doc. 538.

[8] Harvey Lake versus Mexico, NA/RG 76, doc. 607. Lake was first recruited by Vega but later switched to Sánchez Ochoa, Plácido Vega Papers, 2: fol. 448; Samuel Brannan versus Mexico, NA/RG 76, doc. 562.

[9] Deposition of Charles A. Bailey, Harvey Lake versus Mexico, NA/RG, 76, doc. 607; eighteen of the men listed in a dispatch from Mexican consul in San Francisco, California, to Mexican secretary of war, June 14, 1866, copy in NA/RG 76, doc. 904.

Juárez and his following had moved about two hundred fifty miles south to the city of Chihuahua. After resting a week the American soldiers of fortune continued their journey and arrived at the temporary capital of the Mexican republic on September 15.

Captain Lake observed that at Chihuahua the men "were received by the President, and the company was at once accepted in the Mexican service, and known as the American Legion of Honor." [10] A letter from one of the Legionnaires to a friend gives more details about the organization:

> We were well received at Chihuahua, but did not get as high rank as we expected. The President told us that we could have the same rank that we held in our own service, for the present, and that we should remain together five or six months to have an opportunity to learn the language, and then have promotions according to merit. . . .
> Our corps now numbers forty Americans. Each of us has one lancer—a solider with a lance—mounted, who serves us in the capacity of servant and tutor, or instructor in the language. His duty is to take care of our horse and attend to our wants generally, but chiefly to teach us the language.[11]

Soon after the Californians reached Chihuahua other similar groups arrived and were merged into the American Legion of Honor. One such unit, recruited in Texas, was composed of thirteen men under Major George William McNulty. This Civil War veteran, born in Madison County, New York, was twenty-seven years old when he received his commission as a captain with a brevet as major in the Mexican auxiliary army. McNulty's troops were reviewed by Juárez and his staff, and the volunteers were commissioned on September 28, 1866.[12] Major M. K. Young, chief of scouts for Major General Philip Sheridan, recruited another group of about twenty men in New Orleans; they joined the Mexican republican army that same autumn.[13]

In mid-November another contingent of soldiers from California arrived in Chihuahua under command of General Plácido Vega. As pointed out in chapter IV, they had traveled by sea to Topolobampo on the west coast of Mexico, then marched overland approximately three hundred miles to Chihuahua. Vega's Yankee volunteers were mustered into the Legion of Honor, and the Mexican officers and men in his group joined other military units.

Some three weeks before Vega's appearance in the Mexican provisional capital, two talented Yankees, General Lew Wallace and Colonel George Church, had arrived to confer with and aid President Juárez. As will be seen in chapter VII, Wallace was actually a major general in the Mexican army at the time of his visit, having been a secret agent for the Mexican republic for about a year. Colonel Church was a civil engineer who had fought with the 7th and 11th Rhode Island Volunteers in the recent Civil War, and he was a correspondent for the New York *Herald* during his sojourn in Mexico. Both men also represented business interests in New York who wanted concessions in Mexico. Although Wallace and Church did not join the American Legion of Honor, they helped equip the elite unit, for they had just conducted a shipload of arms from New York to Matamoros, Mexico.

After being reviewed and commissioned by Juárez, volunteers in the Legion of Honor marched south to Parral where they joined the central division of the Mexican Army under General Aranda. At their own request the Americans were organized as a separate company and detailed for service independent of the main body of the army.

A unique letter from one of the Legionnaires, written at Nazas, Durango, continues the story and indicates that Colonel Green, original commander of the Legion, was temporarily replaced by another officer:

> After we get below Durango, we expect to have plenty of fighting. General Aranda is in command of the army; he is also appointed Governor of Durango. I like him very much, and he takes a great interest in our corps. By the way, he has . . . assigned his chief of staff, Colonel Arthur Haines, commander of our corps. The appointment meets with our approval, as the Colonel speaks our language fluently, understands all the details of the Mexican service, and is every inch a soldier; he anticipates our wants, asserts our rights and demands for us equal chance with the native officers; in fact he has our utmost confidence.[14]

Supplementary reports state that from Nazas the group advanced upon the city of Durango where they were again put under the command of Colonel George Green.[15]

In January, 1867, the Legion participated in the Battle of Zacatecas where there was a fierce counterattack, and the gallantry of the Americans saved the day according to reports by several of the participants. "Whilst the Mexican soldiers were retreating," wrote one officer, "we dashed into the town and attacked the French Austrian troops . . . and kept them at bay, so that Juárez was enabled to get away in safety, when otherwise he would have been taken." [16] Colonel Church, correspondent for the New York *Herald,* gave his own fast horse to the Mexican president, an act for which he was later given a silver medal by the republican government. Another eyewitness confirmed the report crediting the American Legion with saving the life of Benito Juárez, and he also claimed that they rescued General Aranda's army. "If it had not been for us he would

---

[10] Harvey Lake versus Mexico, NA/RG 76, doc. 607.

[11] San Francisco, *The Daily Times,* January 11, 1867.

[12] George W. McNulty versus Mexico, NA/RG 76, doc. 987; see also his deposition in NA/RG 76, doc. 997.

[13] Sheridan, 1902: 2: pp. 221–222.

[14] Letter published in San Francisco *The Daily Times,* January 11, 1867.

[15] Deposition of G. W. Blasdell, Harvey Lake versus Mexico, NA/RG 76, doc. 607; see also Geo. W. Blasdell versus Mexico, NA/RG 76, doc. 997.

[16] Deposition of G. W. Blasdell, Harvey Lake versus Mexico, NA/RG 76, doc. 607; see also Juárez to Romero, February 22, 1867, Mexico, Legación, 1870–1892: 9: pp. 846–847.

have lost his whole army. We covered his retreat and fought off the pursuers under Miramón."[17] The creditable conduct of the Americans at Zacatecas is also reported by Lieutenant Seaton Schroeder of the United States Navy whose ship was then lying off the Mexican coast. His contemporary published account states that the republican army was saved from pursuit and annihilation only by the brave stand of the Legion of Honor at the defile of Bufa near the city.[18]

During the two-month siege of the city of Querétaro several Legionnaires were captured by the imperialists. One of the American prisoners, Lieutenant George Blasdell, said that on several occasions he was threatened with death "for no other reason than that he was recognized as a citizen of the United States, having been in arms against the so-called Empire of Mexico." Blasdell claimed his life was spared due to the personal intervention of Maximilian.[19] Another American who was imprisoned for two months at Querétaro bitterly observed that he and the Legion of Honor were "placed in a position to do all the hard fighting while the Mexicans gathered the spoils."[20]

Three Mexican armies converged on Maximilian and the defenders of Querétaro in that penultimate climax to the imperial drama. General Mariano Escobedo approached from the east, General Ramón Corona threatened from the south, while General Nicolás Régules and the American Legion advanced from the west. When the city fell on May 15, 1867, the Legion was in the vanguard of the attack, and a number of accounts report that the emperor, white flag in hand, first directed himself to Colonel George Green, commander of the American auxiliary force. The American took Maximilian to General Corona, who in turn sent the royal prisoner on to General Escobedo, commander in chief of the republican armies. According to one author Maximilian gave his sword to Colonel Green, but others state that a subordinate of General Corona received the emperor's weapon and symbol of power.[21]

A letter from the commander of the American Legion of Honor written at Querétaro on the afternoon of that historic day is revealing.

It is with pleasure that I write to let you know that the long war is over. This morning at six o'clock we attacked the place in force, and at eight o'clock we had occupied the principal positions. It was quite cheering to us after having been on the outside for seventy days. We had hardly taken off our clothes during the whole siege, as Maximilian's forces were nearly equal to our own, and we were compelled to be on the watch day and night; but we have had our reward. My small command . . . which composes the Legion of Honor, captured the Carlota Regiment of Cavalry, 500 strong with 80 officers, among them several chiefs. Our victory is complete. We have taken Maximilian, with Miramon and all the principal Generals of the Empire, all the artillery and transportation—in fact, making a clean sweep. We have 10,000 prisoners . . . I have just seen Maximilian, who takes it quite cooly, but says he is Emperor no more.[22]

In the month between the fall of Querétaro and the execution of Maximilian members of the American Legion frequently visited the imprisoned emperor and some of his close advisers. Prince Felix Salm-Salm, a European soldier of fortune on the imperial staff, noted in his diary that Legionnaires offered to help him escape if he would take them all to Europe. He also wrote that the Americans "were highly dissatisfied . . . for they neither received their pay nor their arrears, and were treated in general with contempt, although their services had been found very acceptable."[23] There is also some evidence that Legion officers plotted to free the emperor but were frustrated in their plans by General Escobedo.[24]

The commander of the reserve firing squad at the execution of Maximilian was an American volunteer, Colonel John Sobieski. Ironically this officer had been banished from his European homeland some years before by an order of Maximilian who at that time ruled an Austrian province in northern Italy. After immigrating to the United States, Sobieski fought in the Civil War. In June, 1865, he organized a group of Union veterans to aid Juárez; they went to Mexico via New Orleans and Santa Fé. At Querétaro the American volunteer officer visited the Austrian archduke in his cell and reminded him of the earlier banishment decree.[25]

The day after the execution of Maximilian, President Juárez granted an interview to foreign officers who had served in the republican army. One of those present wrote:

The President won our hearts at once. He warmly thanked us for our services in behalf of Mexico. . . . He said that for Mexicans to fight for Mexico was natural; but for foreigners who had no other ties except the love of liberty and a desire to assist a brave people who were struggling against fearful odds, to make every sacrifice and to suffer every privation for the republic, was a spirit so noble that it could not be put in language.[26]

Although the fall of Querétaro sounded the death knell of the empire, Mexico City still had to be taken. The Legion of Honor went on to the capital where they joined General Porfirio Díaz who was laying siege to the city. Colonel Green first set up his headquarters on Piñon Island in Lake Texcoco where he built a pontoon bridge from the mainland to the island by appropriating 1,600 canal boats. Later when battle conditions per-

---

[17] Deposition of Charles A. Bailey, Harvey Lake versus Mexico, NA/RG 76, doc. 607; Church, 1912: p. xv.
[18] Schroeder, 1887: p. 57.
[19] George W. Blasdell versus Mexico, NA/RG 76, doc. 997.
[20] Joseph H. Blake versus Mexico, NA/RG 76, doc. 904.
[21] Evans, 1870: pp. 228, 231–232; Hobbs, 1875: pp. 306–307; Schroeder, 1887: p. 57.

[22] Col. Green's letter published in *Alta California,* July 3, 1867.
[23] Salm-Salm, 1868: 2: p. 141.
[24] Cornwall, 1871: pp. 447–448.
[25] Sobieski, 1919: p. 4; see also Sobieski [1907]: pp. 119–132.
[26] Sobieski, [1907]: p. 141.

mitted, the Legion moved into the city itself. In one engagement near Chapultepec Castle the Americans crawled up in a ditch to within one hundred yards of the walls of an imperial fortress where, with their Henry rifles, they shot down enemy artillerymen at their posts.[27]

With the liberation of Mexico City in June, 1867, the men in the American Legion of Honor expected to receive their back pay and collect the promised bonuses. Neither was forthcoming. Furthermore, they had to comply with an order for all officers to appear in complete and proper uniforms, and having no money they bought new outfits on credit. After several months of waiting and neglect in the Mexican capital most of the Americans became disgusted and compromised all their claims against Mexico for three hundred dollars in silver, part of which was attached for payment of debts.[28] The release signed by the foreign veterans read in part:

I, a citizen of the United States of America, having served in the Mexican Army, do hereby direct the funding of the bounty of $1,500 in land . . . that I have received from the general Treasury of this nation, the sum of $300 in full payment, hereby renouncing all rights to the said bounty; I further declare that I have received my pay in full, according to my rank, and that I have no right whatever to make any claim against the Mexican Government.[29]

Subsequently many of the men filed suits with the United States–Mexican Claims Commission of 1868, but regardless of the merit of their claims they had legally estopped themselves by signing the above-cited statement.

Most of the Legionnaires had returned to the United States by March, 1868, although their transportation was not furnished by the Mexican government. As one soldier expressed it, "We had to go home to the U.S. as best we could."[30] The commander of the Legion, Colonel George Green, resided in Mexico for the rest of his life and he was in high favor with the Juárez and Díaz administrations. At a state banquet in December, 1869, honoring the Mexican visit of former Secretary of State William H. Seward, Colonel Green was seated near President Juárez, and a reporter noted that Green was "wearing the decoration for the highest order of merit for services rendered in the war against the Empire."[31]

It is difficult to evaluate the contribution of the American Legion of Honor to Mexico's intervention war. Certainly an appraisal by one of the volunteers is highly exaggerated, "but for the American forces forming the Legion of Honor the Republic never would have succeeded." On the other hand, the judgment of another member is exceedingly modest and unrealistic for he wrote, "that having been one of that legion, he leaves it to the justice of the Mexicans themselves to pass upon their usefulness."[32] One important point is that the Legionnaires boosted the morale and firepower of the Juaristas at a critical time when they were initiating their drive south. How can one calculate the psychological and strategic value of American Civil War veterans who served in the Mexican army where they formulated battle plans, serviced artillery pieces, and fought alongside Mexican soldiers? In the engagements they participated in the Americans made a good showing but their numbers were relatively small, and they fought only six months in a seven-years' war. That the American Legion of Honor has been forgotten may be due to its limited accomplishments, or it may be that Mexico, with a plethora of military heroes, would naturally refrain from giving credit to a company of foreign mercenaries. The story of another veteran of the Civil War, General Lew Wallace, who journeyed to Mexico to aid the republican government, will be told in the next chapter.

VII. GENERAL WALLACE—FRIEND OF MEXICO

That Lew Wallace of Indiana was at one time an officer in the Mexican army as well as a secret agent for the Mexican government should be no surprise considering his varied and colorful life as soldier, lawyer, politician, author, and diplomat. Wallace's fame rests on his two best-selling novels, *Ben-Hur* and *The Fair God*, but he was also once an Indiana state senator, a major general in the Union army during the Civil War, governor of the Territory of New Mexico, and United States minister to Turkey. His role in connection with the French intervention in Mexico, while not well known, is no less bizarre than other phases of his career.[1]

Wallace's sympathetic interest in Mexico dated from 1843 when he was enthralled by William H. Prescott's *History of the Conquest of Mexico*. Intermittently for the next thirty years Wallace worked on his first novel, *The Fair God,* based on the clash of Spanish and Indian cultures in Mexico. For years he studied Spanish and tried to read all the material he could find about Mexico. He got his first look at the land of Montezuma in 1846 as a lieutenant in the First Regiment, Indiana Volunteers, during the Mexican War.[2]

---

[27] Evans, 1870: pp. 256–257, 362.
[28] Deposition of G. W. Blasdell in Harvey Lake versus Mexico, NA/RG 76, doc. 607.
[29] Copy of disclaimers in Charles A. Bailey versus Mexico, and Brandt T. Catlin versus Mexico, NA/RG 76, docs. 903, 908.
[30] Deposition of G. W. Blasdell in Harvey Lake versus Mexico, NA/RG 76, doc. 607.
[31] Evans, 1870: p. 279. Green's obituary in Mexico, D.F., *Daily Mexican and Mining Press*, January 16, 1912.

[32] Depositions in Brandt T. Catlin versus Mexico, NA/RG 76, doc. 906.
[1] A preliminary version of this chapter appeared in *Indiana Magazine of History* **59**: pp. 31–50. For biographical data on Wallace see McKee, 1947 and Wallace, 1906.
[2] McKee, 1947: pp. 9–10, 13–17, 122–133.

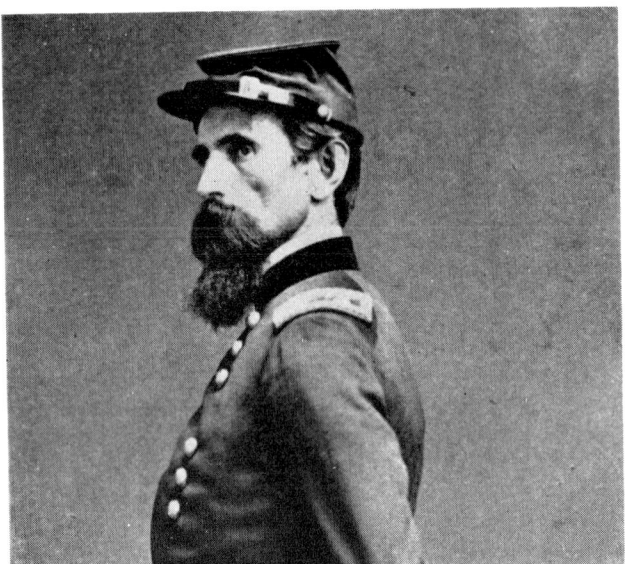

Fig. 7. General Lew Wallace, Hoosier secret agent for Mexico. Photo courtesy of the Indiana Historical Society.

In 1865, after the close of the Civil War, Wallace received a secret assignment and a major general's commission in the Mexican army. In addition to his army salary, he was promised $100,000 for his services to the Mexican republic. Wallace spent the next two years in New York, Washington, Texas, and Mexico working for the Juárez government by giving legal, financial, and military counsel and recruiting volunteers for duty in Mexico.[3]

Wallace's association with the Juárez government began early in 1865 when both the United States and Mexico were convulsed by civil war. The two struggles were interrelated for there was cooperation between the Confederacy and Mexican imperialists while the Union supported Juárez and the Mexican republicans. Through Wallace, who was then a general in the Union army, there was a further relationship; he had a plan to bring the Confederate rebels back into the Union by permitting them to join an American expedition to oust Maximilian and the French troops from Mexico. He visualized a great crusade that would enforce the Monroe Doctrine and unite North and South under one flag. Wallace thought that at least the Trans-Mississippi Department of the Confederacy could be counted on to support such a move.[4]

At the beginning of 1865 the end of the Civil War was in sight, but President Lincoln and his cabinet were worried about affairs in Texas where Confederates, in touch with Mexican imperial troops, were utilizing Mexican ports to outflank the Union blockade. Northern statesmen also feared that some Confederates in desperation might cross into Mexico, take advantage of the disordered conditions there, and continue the war from across the Rio Grande. To pursue such a force might draw the United States into entanglements with European powers and lay the Union open to charges of aggression against a friendly neighbor.

Major General Wallace urged an immediate expedition to Texas, but the president and General Grant opposed Union intervention at that time. Then in a letter to Grant dated January 14, 1865, Wallace asked to be allowed to try his peace plan on the Confederate commanders in Texas. He added, "You know how to get me there—an order to make an inspection of affairs on the Rio Grande will do so." Eight days later Wallace was ordered to "proceed via the Rio Grande to Western Texas, and inspect the conditions of military affairs in that vicinity and on the Rio Grande."[5] The assignment also anticipated a rendezvous with a Mexican republican general for planning concerted action to frustrate any alliance between Confederates and imperialists. Through the Mexican minister to the United States, Wallace received a letter of introduction to General José María Jesús Carvajal, governor of the northeastern Mexican state of Tamaulipas.

Notification of Wallace's mission to the Rio Grande was not communicated to the American secretary of state. "In an interview with President Lincoln on the subject," Wallace recalled, "he admonished me not to mention the business to Mr. Seward."[6] The secretary of state was opposed to any positive step which might serve Napoleon as an excuse for recognizing the Confederacy.

Wallace proceeded to the Mexican frontier by railroad and steamboat to New Orleans. From that city he reported to Grant that Matamoros, Mexico, was to all intents and purposes a rebel port and that there were daily from seventy-five to one hundred and fifty vessels discharging and receiving cargoes at Bagdad, on the Mexican side near the mouth of the Rio Grande. He proposed that Grant give him command of the Department of Texas and asked for an infantry division and a cavalry brigade. The report also noted that plans had been perfected for an interview with Confederate leaders. In New Orleans Wallace withdrew $4,520 in Secret Service funds before boarding the *Clifton* which was put at his disposal for the trip to Brazos de Santiago, Texas.[7] Although Wallace's orders were to proceed via the Rio Grande to western Texas, he found that such a trip was not advisable since the left bank of the river was controlled by Confederates and the right bank by Mexican imperialists. Union forces held only Point Isabel, Texas, near the mouth of the Rio Grande.

---

[3] José M. Carvajal to Wallace, April 26, 1865, Lew Wallace Collection, Indiana Historical Society; McKee, 1947: pp. 95–96; Wallace: 1906: 2, p. 869.

[4] Wallace's notes, March 12, 1865, Lew Wallace Collection.

[5] Wallace, 1906: 2: p. 814; Ulysses S. Grant to Wallace, January 22, 1865, Lew Wallace Collection.

[6] Wallace, 1906: 2: p. 843.

[7] Signed quartermaster vouchers dated February–May, 1865, Lew Wallace Collection. Wallace's report in U.S. War Department, 1880–1901: ser. 1, **48**, 1: pp. 937–938.

Wallace and his staff met with Confederate General James E. Slaughter and his aide, Colonel John S. Ford, at Point Isabel in March, 1865. Negotiations for an exchange of prisoners formed the ostensible reason for this meeting of Union and Confederate officers, but proposals for the pacification of the trans-Mississippi area were discussed along with plans for driving the French out of Mexico.[8] The Southern officers agreed to forward the propositions and terms to their superior, General John G. Walker, then the Confederate military commander of Texas.

In his confidential report to General Grant, Wallace wrote that "both Slaughter and Ford . . . entered heartily into the Mexican project. It is understood between us that the pacification of Texas is the preliminary step to a crossing of the Rio Grande." He also noted that "General Slaughter was of the opinion that the best way for officers in his situation to get honorably back into the Union was to cross the river, conquer two or three states from the French, and ultimately annex them, with all their inhabitants, to the United States."[9]

But the Wallace peace plan was not accepted; moreover, Walker reprimanded Slaughter and reproved Wallace for "seeking an obscure corner of the Confederacy to inaugurate negotiations." Wallace later asserted that Walker's refusal was due to the huge profits the Confederate general was making in cotton by trading with the Galveston blockade runners.[10]

The second phase of Wallace's mission to the Rio Grande involved contacting the Mexican republican forces to ascertain what they would do if Confederate troops crossed over into Mexico in large numbers and joined Maximilian. If the Juaristas would oppose such an invasion, they were to be promised material aid from the United States. The nearest republican officer was General José María Carvajal, governor of the Mexican state of Tamaulipas, and a courier was dispatched to locate him and bring him back if possible. "My messenger found the General in the fastness of the mountains near San Carlos," Wallace wrote, "so reduced that for want of better arms, he was actually practicing his few followers with bows and arrows."[11] Posing as a Texas rancher, the Mexican general slipped through the Imperial lines and came to the boundary where he met with General Wallace late in March, 1865. Carvajal had lived in the United States for some years; he spoke English fluently, and Wallace observed that he "was an American in tastes and ideas."[12]

In the course of the interview with Wallace, Carvajal produced a document from his government naming himself as a commissioner with extensive powers. As will be seen in chapter VIII, this authorization from Juárez empowered Carvajal to purchase 40,000 rifles and other munitions abroad, to enlist up to 10,000 foreigners for service in the Mexican military forces, and to contract for a foreign loan.[13] Upon seeing General Carvajal's commission and being assured that if the Juárez forces were in power they would stop every armed Confederate who attempted to enter Mexico from Texas, Wallace persuaded the Mexican officer to accompany him to Washington. The American agreed to pay for Carvajal's clothes and other expenses and promised to help him in placing a loan and in negotiating the arms purchases. In Carvajal's interest, Wallace noted:

> It was very desirable, for a time, at least, to conceal his departure; at the same time, it was of absolute importance to me personally that the intrigue I was inaugurating should be covered up as effectually as possible; so the General took the name of "Mr. Joseph Smith," by which he continued to be known in Washington and New York.[14]

By the time the two generals arrived at the American capital late in April, 1865, Lincoln had been assassinated, Lee had surrendered to Grant, and the American Civil War was rapidly drawing to a close. General Wallace was detailed to serve on the court-martial board for the trial of those implicated in the plot to assassinate Lincoln, Grant, and Seward, and was thus occupied for the next two months.

Nevertheless on April 26, 1865, Carvajal offered Wallace, upon his impending resignation from the United States Army, a commission as a major general in the Mexican army. Wallace was to be paid $100,000, and his duties were to put the Mexican general in touch with persons able to help him financially, to assist him in procuring munitions, and to organize and lead a corps of American volunteers who would serve under the flag of the Mexican republic. According to Wallace this agreement with Carvajal was sanctioned by Grant with whom he conferred before accepting the offer.[15]

Wallace subsequently arranged a conference with Carvajal and introduced him to a fellow Hoosier, General Herman Sturm. The three generals conferred on the plan to raise an auxiliary force of ten thousand Americans, and Sturm, chief of ordnance for the state of Indiana, was commissioned by Carvajal to procure

---

[8] Wallace's proposition outlined in his memo dated March 12, 1865, Lew Wallace Collection. Point Isabel is now called Port Isabel.

[9] Confidential report, Wallace to Grant, March 14, 1865, *ibid.*; see also official report of same date. Letters cited from Wallace refer, unless otherwise indicated, to draft or retained copies.

[10] John G. Walker to Wallace, March 25 and Wallace to Grant, April 18, 1865, *ibid.* Slaughter later joined the imperialists in Mexico and warned them of Wallace's plans, Rippy, 1926: p. 244.

[11] Wallace to American–Mexican Claims Commission, November 25, 1869, Lew Wallace Collection. The original petition in NA/RG 76, doc. 425.

[12] Wallace, 1906: 2: p. 869.

[13] Carvajal's commission is printed in U.S. Congress, *House Exec. Doc. 33*, pp. 112-113. See also Mexico, Legación, *Responsabilidades*, 1867: p. 24.

[14] Wallace to American–Mexican Claims Commission, November 25, 1869, Lew Wallace Collection.

[15] José M. Carvajal to Wallace, April 26, 1865, *ibid.*; Wallace, 1906: 2: p. 869; McKee, 1947: pp. 95-96.

the necessary military supplies and to provide for transportation and care of the foreign legionnaires until they reached Mexico. The American volunteer corps, composed primarily of recently discharged veterans, was to assemble somewhere on the Rio Grande. In order to circumvent neutrality laws these men would be organized as emigration societies.[16]

Hoping to establish chapters "in every country town," Wallace organized the Mexican Aid Society to raise funds and recruit soldiers for the contemplated expedition. He wrote to friends asking their help in organizing branch clubs that would:

control public sentiment, govern the politicians, raise funds, recruit soldiers, and beget cooperation and united intelligent management. Any number of veterans will wish to go to Mexico as soon as they are somewhat wearied of the monotony of home. They will want to know how to get there. These societies will show them the way and afford information generally.[17]

About this time General Sheridan was put in command of the United States Army corps along the Rio Grande, a position that Wallace had requested for himself so that he could organize and direct the projected brigade of American volunteers to Mexico. In June, 1865, Wallace was again passed over when General Schofield was selected to command the projected army of Union and Confederate veterans destined for Mexico. According to Schofield, this decision was made at a Washington conference attended by President Johnson, Secretary Seward, Secretary Stanton, General Grant, General Schofield, and Mexican Minister Romero. Both Grant and Romero were acquainted with the Wallace-Carvajal project, but Grant mistrusted Wallace and feared that under him the enterprise would end discredited. Romero urged that Wallace be put in charge until the group crossed into Mexico when Schofield would take command.[18]

While negotiations were going on regarding Schofield's command in the Southwest and his later reassignment to Europe, General Wallace continued with his own plans to enlist a corps of American veterans for service in Mexico. He wrote a number of his army officer friends in various localities asking them to recruit soldier-emigrants for the projected expedition. In the first part of September, 1865, Wallace noted in a letter to his wife that he had men "all ready and was waiting only for the means."[19] Later, in a note to General John W. Geary asking him to organize men in Pennsylvania, Wallace reported that arrangements had been made for nine other states. General James P. Brownlow was in charge of Tennessee, Colonel W. E. Woodruff of Kentucky, General Thomas O. Osborne of Illinois, Generals Robert S. Foster and John Coburn of Indiana, General Erastus B. Tyler of Ohio, General Maxwell Z. Woodhull of Maine, and Colonel Lionel A. Sheldon of Louisiana. Confederate officers were also involved in the widespread scheme; Colonel John S. Mosby was to forward emigrants from Virginia while Colonel John S. Ford, the officer Wallace had met at Point Isabel, was to direct recruiting in Texas.[20]

One of Wallace's most active agents was a former Confederate officer, Colonel H. Clay Crawford, who was not only eager to lead a brigade into Mexico but was also willing to use some of his own money for the organization. On November 4, 1865, Crawford was sent to the Rio Grande with a set of orders from General Wallace. In Brownsville, Texas, he was to get in touch with Mexican Colonel Andreas Treviño, then organize one thousand men and encamp them on the river above Brownsville. Some of the units already formed, such as that of Colonel Ford, were to be incorporated into the brigade. Crawford was instructed not to open negotiations with the Mexican republican leaders; nor was he to cross the river until the arrival of Wallace or General Carvajal. He was informed that arms, uniforms, and other provisions would be forthcoming. Wallace wrote to General Grant informing him of Crawford's mission and asking that some of the arms at New Orleans be made available for the brigade.[21]

When he arrived on the Rio Grande, Crawford had difficulty enlisting recruits. There was a lack of money to advance salaries and bonuses and to outfit the men. Wallace was not able to send the promised supplies because the Mexican bond issue that he and Carvajal had been negotiating proved a failure. But Crawford and his second in command, Colonel Arthur L. Reed, did gather a few followers, some of them Negroes, and they prepared for an offensive. It was reported that Crawford was offering fifty dollars per month to all those who joined his corps.[22]

In the first part of January, 1866, Crawford decided to move across the Rio Grande and capture the town of Bagdad at the mouth of the great river. This action, of course, violated Wallace's instructions as well as international law, but one of his motives was to liberate seventeen of his men who had been captured by the Mexican imperialist commander at Bagdad, General Tomás Mejia. These prisoners were under death sentence in accordance with the infamous "Black Flag" decree of Emperor Maximilian which called for the execution of all those caught fighting against the empire. The fact that these prisoners were in Mexico would indicate that Crawford or his men had crossed the river

---

[16] Sturm, 1869: pp. 2–4. Sturm's commission, dated May 1, 1865, obliged him to resign from his Indiana state position.
[17] Wallace to Thomas Buchanan Read, April 30, 1865, Lew Wallace Collection.
[18] Schofield, *Forty-Six Years,* 1897: pp. 379–380; Mexico, Legación, 1870–1892: 5: p. 722.
[19] Wallace to his wife, September 4, 1865, Lew Wallace Collection.

[20] Wallace to John W. Geary [September, 1865], *ibid.*
[21] Wallace to R. Clay Crawford, November 4, 1865, and Wallace to Ulysses S. Grant, November 16, 1865, *ibid.*
[22] Domenech, 1866: p. 39.

on a previous sortie. In any event, on the first of January, Crawford wrote to General Godfrey Weitzel, the ranking United States Army officer in Texas, asking him to intercede on behalf of the prisoners; Weitzel's request for clemency however, was not granted.[23]

The attack on Bagdad, generally characterized as North American in concept and execution, had Mexican planning, approval, and cooperation. One Mexican historian, Niceto de Zamacois, does state that Colonel Reed discussed at length the Bagdad plan of attack with General Escobedo, chief republican military officer in northern Mexico.[24] Colonel Enrique Mejía, not to be confused with the imperial general, Tomás Mejía, was cognizant of the Bagdad plans, and with Escobedo's approval he was to become military commandant of the town once Crawford's men had liberated it.

On January 5 at about four o'clock in the morning, Lieutenant Colonel Edmundo Davis, commander of the 118th Colored Battallion, United States forces, crossed the river at the head of about one hundred of his men and some twenty or thirty soldiers of fortune including Crawford and Reed. The force surprised the Mexican imperial guard of about two hundred men, took them prisoner, and began to sack the town; wholesale looting then broke out. Seven witnesses later declared that Colonel Davis was drunk at the time and that he returned to his base leaving the town in the hands of the adventurers who had accompanied him and of others who arrived after the capitulation.[25]

The following day Colonel Enrique Mejía with 200 volunteers, presumably Mexican republican exiles, crossed the river and took over as military commandant of Bagdad. He had to overcome the strenuous opposition of Crawford and Reed who momentarily made Mejía and his officers prisoners. The French ship *Antonia* appeared off Bagdad on January 6, 1866, and opened fire on Crawford's men killing two of the Negroes. The land force lacked artillery, but they returned fire on the vessel and evened the score by mortally wounding a French corporal and an Austrian sergeant. At this juncture American merchants of the town sent strong protests to General Weitzel across the river; they feared a further loss of real estate and merchandise through looting and warfare. Colonel Mejía also appealed to the American general for assistance.[26]

General Weitzel, observing the anarchy that followed the capture of Bagdad, decided to intervene with federal troops. Colonel Hudson was dispatched to the city with 150 Negro troops and instructions to restore order. This only served to complicate matters since Hudson's men promptly united with Crawford. Weitzel then saw that he would have to move across the river in strength and, on January 13, he went to Bagdad, promptly established military law, curbed the excesses, and restored order. Crawford was arrested and sent to Fort Jackson, Louisiana, and his men were returned to the American side of the river.[27]

But the confusion in Bagdad continued because the Mexican republican leaders and local politicians fought each other. By January 17, Colonel Mejía was forced out as military commandant due to squabbles between Mexican generals and demagogues, one of who wanted the adventurer Reed appointed as commandant.[28]

When elements of the French Gulf Fleet appeared in the harbor and protested the occupation of the Mexican city by the United States Army, the Bagdad affair ended about as swiftly as it had began. Weitzel, who most certainly had orders to avert war with the French, withdrew his force to Brownsville, and the imperialist troops moved back into Bagdad on January 24, 1866.[29] Thus ended the three-week interlude of nominal rule by the Mexican republicans, both aided and impeded by regular and irregular American troops.

The raid on Bagdad irritated General Wallace and it delayed his Mexican plans. In a letter to Carvajal about Crawford he understated the case:

The newspaper reports satisfy me that he is not the man for delicate duty he was assigned to. Yet we had no choice —he only had the money. If he should succeed, he will have lost the advantages of a surprise. Let him go on, however. All eyes will be centered on him there, leaving us comparatively free from espionage here.[30]

Crawford was later released from custody, and he sent Wallace a full report of the Bagdad melee along with a bill for $122,000 as compensation for his services. Wallace, who refused to answer the report, was embarrassed and angry over the incident which he said was due to Crawford's "stupidity, madness, and gross violation of instructions." Nevertheless, he suggested to Carvajal that they take no action against Crawford "until we are in your country, when you can act as justice dictates, free from danger of law suits, etc. . . ."[31]

Undaunted by the experience of Crawford's raiders and optimistic over the prospect of a Mexican loan being guaranteed by the United States, General Wallace continued to make plans for a large military expedition which he would lead into Mexico. He renewed his contacts with the emigration societies and organized three

---

[23] Domenech, 1868: 2: p. 374.
[24] Zamacois, 1877–1882: 18: p. 339.
[25] Enrique A. Mejía to Mariano Escobedo, January 10, 1866, Enrique Antonio Mejía Papers, Part II, box 1, fol. 98, Bancroft Library. Letters from Mejía refer to draft copies.
[26] Enrique A. Mejía to Mariano Escobedo, January 9, 1866; Mejía to Godfrey Weitzel, January 13, 1866, Mejía Papers, Part II, box 1, fol. 92, 114. See also Domenech, 1868: 3: p. 375.

[27] Domenech, 1868: 3: pp. 376–377.
[28] Enrique A. Mejía to Matías Romero, January 17, 1866, Mejía Papers, Part II, box 1, fol. 121.
[29] Adolfo Garza to Enrique A. Mejía, January 25, 1866, *ibid.*, fol. 133.
[30] Wallace to José M. Carvajal, January 11, 1866, Lew Wallace Collection.
[31] Same to same, January 24, 1866, *ibid.*

brigades of infantry in Illinois, Indiana, and Tennessee. The groups had a dichotomous designation; privately they were brigades, but publicly they were known as the Order of Miamis, an Association of Emigrants. In the manner of a number of clubs and fraternal groups there were code names for the various elements within the organization. Armories were referred to as "wigwams"; companies, named after the counties, were "tribes"; and the officers were "sachems," "chiefs," "braves," and "runners." Although the Miamis had initiation fees and dues, Wallace had to advance about $5,000 for the project.[32]

During the spring of 1866 Wallace, Carvajal, and Sturm made plans for a new military offensive on the Rio Grande. Because of numerous reports of factions and personal feuds among republican leaders of that area, Romero and Grant urged Carvajal to return to his homeland and try to reconcile the factions. Sturm promised to send him military supplies and Wallace agreed to provide American auxiliary troops. Within a short time after his arrival Carvajal consolidated his position and became master of the border towns near the mouth of the Rio Grande. On June 23, he reported that he was in control of Matamoros, rendezvous city for the expedition that Wallace and Sturm were preparing.[33]

Wallace then alerted officers of the Order of Miamis about the projected campaign. In a letter to General Thomas Osborn he stated that he expected to have five thousand men on the way to Mexico within the week. In a subsequent note, dated July 14, 1866, he ordered Osborn to start moving his men. "Do not wait for arms . . . send your men forward . . . in squads of eight or ten."[34] Although the recruits were directed to go first to New Orleans and then to Matamoros, only a few of the Miamis ever made it to Mexico. True, all of the members wanted to help liberate Mexico from the foreign invader, but only if their salary and reimbursement for equipment and transportation were advanced. Neither Wallace nor Osborn, nor any other "sachem" provided that essential element.

Meanwhile, in New York, General Sturm chartered the steamship *J. W. Everman* for the trip to Mexico and loaded it with sufficient arms to equip 7,000 soldiers. How he did it on credit for Mexican bonds will be seen in chapter IX. The expedition sailed from New York City on July 26, 1866, with Wallace in charge of the volatile cargo. Several Mexican army officers returned to their country aboard the ship and the passengers included seven citizens of the United States. The latter were part of the Wallace-Sturm-Carvajal coterie, including Colonel George Earl Church, a correspondent for the New York *Herald*; Wilbur F. Stocking, agent for the firm negotiating Mexican bonds; and Herman Sturm's brother, Captain Frederick C. Sturm.[35]

Writing to his wife while aboard ship, Wallace was apprehensive. He noted that "the question close upon us is: Can I succeed in landing in Matamoras [*sic*] the *material*—contraband with the French—now in our ship's hold?"[36] The answer was soon forthcoming, for after the cargo was transferred to a river steamer and then unloaded on the Matamoros levee, a local revolt against Carvajal occurred. In this tumult the munitions were pillaged, the Yankees jailed, and Carvajal went into hiding in Texas. Later the new commander, Servando Canales, released the men and permitted some of the munitions to be transferred to the other side of the river for warehousing. Louis Avery, United States vice-consul at Matamoros, told Wallace that the revolt had originated among Carvajal's subordinates and against the wishes of Canales. He reported that Carvajal was a despotic ruler, giving too many concessions to Americans and underpaying his army.[37]

From Matamoros, Wallace, Church, and Stocking traveled overland to Monterrey, Mexico, where they hoped Juárez's commander-in-chief, General Mariano Escobedo, would accept the arms and sign receipts for the merchandise. After a month of preliminaries with Escobedo during which his agent agreed to take 1,000 rifles, 345 pistols, 6 artillery pieces, and other munitions,[38] Wallace and Church decided to go on to the city of Chihuahua where Juárez and the central government were located. It was a twenty-day journey in the carriage supplied by General Escobedo, and along the way they looked over some of the silver mines of northern Mexico.

In Chihuahua, temporary capital of the Mexican republic, the Americans met with Juárez and his cabinet and submitted a written report on the *Everman* expedition. In the months that followed, Church, a civil and military engineer, and Wallace, the soldier-lawyer, tried to get mining, colonization, banking, and telegraph concessions from the republican government. Draft propositions in Wallace's papers indicate that a number of American capitalists were behind the schemes. Cyrus W. Field, president of the Atlantic Telegraph Company, David Hoadley, president of the Panama Railroad Company, and General E. S. Sanford, vice-president of the Adams Express Company, are but three of the names mentioned in the documents.[39] Wallace's opinion of the Mexican officials was revealed in a letter to his wife:

The attaches of this government here, from Juárez down, are very polite and kind to me. My opinion of the former

---

[32] McKee, 1947: p. 103; constitution and initiation ceremony of Order of Miamis in notebooks, Lew Wallace Collection.

[33] Wallace, 1906: 2: pp. 871, 873.

[34] Wallace to Thomas Osborn, July 12, 14, 1866, Lew Wallace Collection.

[35] Sturm, 1872: pp. 25–26; NA/RG 76, docs. 673, 763; McKee, 1947: p. 104.

[36] Wallace, 1906: 2: p. 874.

[37] Wilbur Stocking to Herman Sturm, August 13, 1866, in Sturm, 1872: pp. 39–40; see McKee, 1947: p. 105.

[38] Mexico, Legación, *Circulares*, 1868: 1: pp. 475–476.

[39] Draft proposals, Wallace to Benito Juárez, October 22, 1866, Lew Wallace Collection.

grows better every day. Without doubt, he is really a great man in the true sense of the words. I wish we had as good a one at the head of our government. And as to his cabinet, I think I told you it was composed of abler men than ours. I have seen a good deal of them lately, and what I thought before, I am sure of now.[40]

With the resurgence of the republican forces and the concomitant collapse of Maximilian's empire, the Juárez cabinet moved back toward central Mexico. Wallace and Church accompanied the Juaristas on the 450-mile trek to Durango, but when the officials moved farther south to Zacatecas, Wallace returned to the United States and arrived in Indiana in February, 1867. He had been in Mexico almost seven months, and, in addition to the partial fiasco of the *Everman* expedition, his plans for concessions had been thwarted or at least delayed in the classical *mañana* manner. Colonel Church remained in Mexico until May, reporting for the New York *Herald* and helping Juárez's minister of war plan the closing campaigns of the conflict.[41]

Meanwhile, Wilbur Stocking returned to Brownsville, Texas, where he turned over the munitions to a local firm that arranged for their ultimate sale to Juarist commanders. The governor of Coahuila and the commander of Tampico received the bulk of the arms, amounting to more than 3,000 rifles, 500 pistols, 250 sabers, 1,000,000 percussion caps, and 274,000 cartridges.[42] Although the *Everman* expedition was in many ways a misfortune, it did result in the delivery to the Mexican republicans of a considerable quantity of first-rate arms and ammunition.

About the time of Maximilian's surrender in May, 1867, Lew Wallace resigned his commission as an army officer and agent of the Mexican republic. He spent parts of the next two years in Mexico trying to get cash compensation or a business or mining concession in exchange for Carvajal's written promise of $100,000. Carvajal himself was out of favor with the Juárez administration and in exile in the United States. Wallace accepted $2,500 from Romero in 1868, but he maintained that this was only partial payment on account. In a later suit, the United States–Mexican Claims Commission of 1868–1876 ruled against Wallace's petition for $25,552.50 on the grounds that Carvajal had exceeded his authority in the contracts he made with Wallace. Finally, in 1882, the Mexican government paid Wallace $15,000, a sum considerably less than the amount promised by Carvajal, but one accepted as payment in full by the Hoosier general.[43]

What did Lew Wallace accomplish as an agent of the Mexican republic during the French intervention in that country? One important contribution was that he enthusiastically lent his name to the cause of the Mexican republic, thereby giving that government added popularity and respectability in the United States. In the field of propaganda Wallace established chapters of the Mexican Aid Society, which raised money for Juárez and kept the issue of French violation of the Monroe Doctrine before the American public. Although he agreed to organize and lead a large expeditionary force of volunteers to Mexico, this foreign legion never assembled because of opposition by the United States secretary of state coupled with a lack of financial support. Wallace's recruiting activities, while abortive with respect to the large expedition, did result in a number of the volunteers crossing into Mexico individually and in small groups. Through Wallace, General Herman Sturm was employed by the Mexican republic as an expediter of military supplies. Wallace later noted that in the closing battles of the war in Mexico two of the armies, "the most important, that of Díaz and that of Escobedo, were in great part equipped by Sturm and I. . . ."[44] By bringing to Washington and New York General José Carvajal, who had broad powers from his government, Wallace served as a catalyst in the important financial and logistic negotiations that led to succor for the Juárez forces. The activities of General Carvajal will be outlined in the following chapter.

VIII. GENERAL CARVAJAL—AUTOCRAT OF THE RIO GRANDE

The Mexican secret agent who audaciously attempted to float a loan of $30,000,000 in the United States and to recruit 10,000 Americans for the Mexican army was General José María de Jesús Carvajal, governor of the state of Tamaulipas. He was also the man who gave Mexican army commissions to the American generals Lew Wallace and Herman Sturm, engaging them for service to the Juárez administration. Although Carvajal exceeded the broad powers granted him and was later repudiated by his government, his activities in the United States during the French intervention are significant because they resulted in a substantial amount of material aid being sent to Mexico from its northern neighbor.

Carvajal was born in 1810, the same year that Mexico's revolt against Spain began; during the following fifty years he was linked with a number of political revolts and plots that characterized the era. Young Carvajal spent his early years at the family home in Soto la Marina, Tamaulipas. Later he was sent to the United States for his education; he graduated from Bethany College, Virginia (now West Virginia), where he learned to speak and write English fluently. When he returned home, he served in the Mexican navy for a

---

[40] Wallace to his wife, October 5, 1866 [a.l.s.], *ibid.*
[41] Church, 1912: p. xv.
[42] Mexico, Legación, *Circulares*, 1868: 1: pp. 475–476.
[43] Wallace to American–Mexican Claims Commission, November 25, 1869, Lew Wallace Collection; U.S. Congress, *Senate Exec. Doc. 31*, pp. 38–39; McKee, 1947: pp. 112–113.

[44] Wallace, 1906: 2: p. 872.

Fig. 8. General José María Carvajal, Mexican secret agent in the United States. Photo courtesy of the Indiana Historical Society.

few years and was decorated with the Cross of Honor in 1836 during the Texas war for independence.[1]

A long army career began when Carvajal was commissioned as a lieutenant in 1838. The following year he fought against French troops in the "Pastry War," and during the Mexican-American War he served as a captain in the army at Veracruz and later in the guerrilla forces of Eulalio Villas. In the 1855 revolution of Ayutla, aimed at overthrowing the dictatorship of Santa Anna, Carvajal was a general in the liberal forces fighting in the northern states of Mexico. By the time of the War of the Reform, in which he operated under General Santos Degollado, Carvajal had become a political force in the struggle for control of the state of Tamaulipas.[2]

When the French troops intervened in Mexico in 1862, José Carvajal gathered together an army to defend the Huasteca, that region lying between and in the states of Tamaulipas, Veracruz, and San Luis Potosí. With a force of about 1,200 men Carvajal defeated imperialist Colonel Manuel Llorente in a battle for the port of Tuxpan. Later he joined forces with his former opponent, Juan N. Cortina, serving under the latter in campaigns against French forces. Subsequently Cortina went over to the Maximilian side and turned on Carvajal and other republican leaders.[3]

As regular armies of the Mexican republic were defeated by imperial and French troops, their leaders imprisoned and the men scattered, resistance continued in the form of guerrilla warfare. Mexican *guerrilleros* knew the resources and geography of their area; moreover, they could be subsistence farming one day, fighting the next, then be peace-loving farmers again by hiding their rifles or machetes. To combat Mexican bush fighters who continued to resist, Colonel Charles Dupin organized the Contre-Guérilla Française. Dupin concentrated his activities in the Huasteca region, seeking out *guerrilleros* in their most remote positions. Carvajal was one of the important guerrilla leaders; his strategy was to withdraw into the mountains after striking the enemy in the forts and cities. One of Colonel Dupin's subordinates recorded that the Mexican officer was known for his valor, intelligence, and honesty. He also noted that Carvajal was a great admirer of North Americans and that there were Texans and French deserters in his force along with the core of Tamaulipecos. The Contre-Guérilla outfought Carvajal's group in several engagements, and they penetrated into mountain hideouts to capture Mexicans and their equipment. The French had a good intelligence system that included Carvajal's cousin, Don Jesús de la Serna, who passed on information about the location and strength of the Mexican guerrillas.[4]

By the end of 1864 Carvajal and about three hundred followers were in the mountains near the Texas border without sufficient manpower or munitions to initiate an offensive military action. It appeared to Carvajal that only with aid from abroad would the Mexican republicans be able to win victories and again control their country. Therefore, the titular governor of Tamaulipas sent his friend, Ramírez Arellano, to Chihuahua with a petition asking the Juárez cabinet for permission and authority to seek military help outside the republic. Earlier Carvajal had made a similar request at Monterrey when the cabinet was established there.[5]

The representative brought back a commission from the supreme government, dated November 12, 1864, granting broad powers to General Carvajal. He was authorized to enlist from 1,000 to 10,000 foreigners for service in the Mexican army and he could purchase 40,000 rifles and 3,000 assorted arms as well as batteries of artillery and a substantial amount of ammunition. Another provision of his special orders permitted Carvajal to negotiate a public loan abroad in the amount he considered necessary to defray expenses of the foreign legionnaires, including payment of their salaries for two years. To pay for the munitions and to guarantee the loan, Carvajal was authorized to pledge the revenues of the state of Tamaulipas granting interest at six

---

[1] Carvajal's military personnel file, *expediente* XI/III/1-38, fol. 2, 5, 193, Archivo Histórico Militar, Secretaría Defensa Nacional, Mexico (ADN).

[2] *Ibid.*, fol. 3–4. See also Ocampo, 1900–1901: 2: pp. LXII, LXV.

[3] Kératry, 1868: p. 110.

[4] Bancroft, 1888: 6: pp. 112–113, 119; Kératry, 1868: pp. 278–279.

[5] Mexico, Legación, *Responsabilidades*, 1887: p. 303; Sturm, 1869: p. 26.

per cent per year until the contracts or loans were repaid.[6]

Although he had broad powers, General Carvajal at first held his commission in abeyance because he considered it too limited. Even though he could legally hypothecate the income of his state, in actuality he had no control over it since the major revenue sources were customhouses under the French tricolor. As for raising the 10,000 man foreign corps, the American Civil War precluded successful recruitment in the United States at that time. Nor was a Mexican loan apt to be successful owing to the precarious position of the Mexican republican government and competing opportunities for investment.

As noted in the previous chapter, Carvajal was still in his mountain bivouac in the spring of 1865 when a messenger from General Lew Wallace arrived with a note suggesting a meeting on the Rio Grande. The two generals met at Brazos de Santiago, Texas, and when Wallace saw Carvajal's commission from the Juárez government, he thought that the document would enable the Mexican to secure assistance from the United States. Their clandestine meeting took place at the end of March, 1865, when recent Union victories had assured a prompt end to the War of the Rebellion and chances for aid to Mexico from the United States looked promising. Wallace probably saw himself as the officer in charge of the 10,000 man foreign legion; no doubt Carvajal concurred.

Wallace persuaded Carvajal to accompany him to New York and Washington where he promised to help him float a loan and secure munitions. In the latter part of April, 1865, Carvajal had a series of interviews with Matías Romero, the Mexican minister in Washington. At first Romero was enthusiastic, but eventually he became skeptical of Carvajal's confidence in the success of a Mexican loan. According to Romero, Carvajal believed that citizens of the United States were so sympathetic to the cause of the Mexican republic that they would give financial aid without concern for the conditions under which the aid was rendered. Romero also noted that the Tamaulipas governor thought that wealthy Americans were not only willing but anxious to give resources to Mexico; thus Carvajal proposed to negotiate a large loan. Romero astutely observed that "the raising of a Mexican loan in this country was a hard business . . . which would require work, the cooperation of men of affairs, and a combination of favorable circumstances."[7]

Before proceeding to New York, then as now financial center of the United States, Carvajal engaged two Union generals for service with the Mexican army. Lew Wallace agreed to accept a general's commission with command of a corps of American volunteers in Mexico, while one of Wallace's Hoosier friends, Herman Sturm, was employed by Carvajal as purchasing agent for the Mexican republic. Sturm immediately set to work to purchase the requisite munitions for a unit of 10,000 volunteers, but Wallace was not able to give full time to the scheme until he resigned his United States Army commission in the fall of 1865.

Meanwhile, General Carvajal went to New York on June 1, where he attempted to raise funds for munitions and for the contemplated foreign legion. On the tenth of the following month he wrote to the Mexican minister saying that he had despaired of raising money and asked for a loan of two thousand dollars to enable him to return to Tamaulipas immediately. However, three days later Carvajal reported from New York that "a strong company of that city offered to lend him two millions of dollars in cash, all of the war material he wanted, and ample facilities to raise means on the largest scale."[8]

Late in July, Carvajal wired Wallace to meet him in New York to draw up an important financial contract. The two generals met in Carvajal's room in the Union Place Hotel. Also at the rendezvous was a New York lawyer, Daniel Woodhouse, secretary and financial agent of the United States, European, and West Virginia Land and Mining Company. Carvajal attested to Woodhouse's character, and he showed Wallace a prospectus of the aforesaid company which listed its liquid assets at $20,000,000 and gave the names of several prominent men as officers of the company and backers of the enterprise.[9]

Wallace drafted a contract between General Carvajal acting for the United States of Mexico, and Daniel Woodhouse, secretary of the United States, European, and West Virginia Land and Mining Company. The contract was dated as if executed at San Carlos, Mexico, on May 15, 1865, when in reality it was signed in New York City about July 24, 1865. By terms of this agreement the company was to negotiate the sale of $30,000,000 worth of interest-bearing Mexican bonds in return for certain concessions. The bonds were guaranteed by 500,000 acres of select mineral lands and 5,000,000 acres of select agricultural lands in the Mexican states of Tamaulipas and San Luis Potosí, as well as by eighty per cent of all federal and state revenues of those states, estimated at $3,000,000 annually. The company was granted 2,169,232 acres of vacant agricultural land in the two Mexican states as well as 2,136 mining sites. The mines were to be selected by company agents; according to mining laws of Mexico each site was equivalent to about fifty acres.[10]

One of the major clauses of the Woodhouse-Carvajal contract dealt with concessions for building railroad and

---

[6] Carvajal's commission in U.S. Congress, *House Exec. Doc. 33*, pp. 112–113.

[7] Mexico, Legación, *Circulares*, 1868: 1: p. 307.

[8] Romero to Lerdo de Tejada, Washington, July 25, 1865, U.S. Congress, *House Exec. Doc. 33*, p. 21.

[9] McKee, 1947: p. 97.

[10] Carvajal-Woodhouse contract, U.S. Congress, *House Exec. Doc. 33*, pp. 24–30; see also Frazer, "The United States," 1944: pp. 28–40.

telegraph lines in Mexico. Carvajal granted the company an exclusive right-of-way and privilege of constructing and operating a double-track railroad from Matamoros to the western limit of the state of San Luis Potosí. Branch lines to Tampico and Soto la Marina were also authorized, and General Carvajal pledged himself "to exert all his influence and interest" in persuading the Mexican government to grant similar terms for the extension of the railroad to Mazatlán. The company agreed to transport, free of charge, military troops and munitions of war during the thirty-five-year monopoly period.[11]

As for the $30,000,000 in Mexican bonds, they were to be issued in $50, $100, $500, and $1,000 denominations and pay seven per cent interest semi-annually. The bonds could be discounted as much as sixty per cent, and the company was to receive five per cent commission on all sales. If the bonds sold for any amount over sixty cents in gold to the dollar in bonds, the company would receive a thirty per cent commission on the excess realized on the sale. Proceeds from sales of all bonds were to be deposited in the Bank of Commerce of the City of New York for the use of the republican government of Mexico.[12]

On August 6, Carvajal submitted the contract to the Mexican minister, who refused to ratify it. Indeed, Romero immediately wrote to his government that Carvajal had exceeded his powers, and in commenting on the contract he said, "in my judgment it is simply granting the corporation very valuable privileges, for the only consideration of selling our bonds at a very low figure."[13]

Woodhouse and Carvajal signed a second contract which was to be kept secret because its provisions might contravene United States neutrality laws. Under this agreement the company would turn over to Carvajal $3,000,000 in cash the moment the first contract was signed. The Mexican general had been advised not to sign or deliver either of the contracts until the money had been advanced, but he was outwitted by a simple stratagem. Woodhouse purloined the first signed document from the notary; he then refused to execute the second contract and advance the stipulated sum.[14]

It soon developed that Carvajal, Wallace, and Sturm had been completely deceived by Woodhouse. The company he represented, the United States, European, and West Virginia Land and Mining Company, which was supposed to have a capital of $20,000,000, was entirely unknown to the business world, and it had no funds in the Howes and Macy bank, announced in the prospectus as its bankers, nor in the hands of the company treasurer. Reputable persons whose names appeared in the prospectus declared that they did not know Mr. Woodhouse, or that he had used their name without their consent or knowledge. And Daniel Woodhouse, principal figure and almost the only partner in the corporation, "'seemed to be a lawyer of the lowest class, without any pecuniary responsibility, and with a reputation sufficiently bad to ruin any respectable business in which he took a part."[15] When the truth about Woodhouse's company became known, General Sturm observed that "Carvajal had been made the victim of a parcel of speculative rogues."[16]

Woodhouse then offered to reorganize the company, promising that some highly respectable New Yorkers, including Cornelius Vanderbilt, Moses H. Grinnell, and the former governor, Edwin D. Morgan, would participate. Generals Wallace, Sturm, and Carvajal attended the reorganization meeting held on August 31, 1865, but the reputable financiers did not appear. Wallace characterized the meeting as a "decided failure," and that same day he wrote Romero:

> The fiasco of the United States, European, and West Virginia Land and Mining Company is complete; but thank Heaven, it has resulted in two things: the bonds are engraved, and willing men stand ready to put them in the market *couleur de rose*. I feel no disposition to despair; far from it. . . . Please consider me fully committed to your cause. . . .[17]

Although Carvajal and the Mexican minister denounced the contract as being null and void and revoked the power of attorney given Woodhouse to have the bonds printed, Woodhouse continued to regard the contract as valid. For more than two years he tried to force the Mexican government to allow his concessions. The name of the company was changed several times, once to the National American and Mexican Company, then later to the American and Mexican International Company, and new officers were appointed from time to time, usually without the knowledge or consent of those so elected. By this method Romero was named vice-president of the company in December, 1865, but he immediately declined the office and restated his position that the contract was invalid. Romero's argument was threefold: Carvajal had exceeded his powers by making grants of railroads for which he had no authority, Woodhouse misrepresented the assets and capabilities of his company, and the laws of New York would not permit the company to negotiate Mexican bonds, build railroads in Mexico, and operate mines outside the state of New York.[18]

Of course Woodhouse could have been arrested and probably convicted for his fraudulent activities, but Wallace and Carvajal decided against taking any legal

---

[11] U.S. Congress, *House Exec. Doc. 33*, pp. 25–36.
[12] *Ibid.*, pp. 27–28.
[13] Romero to Minister of Foreign Relations, New York, August 8, 1865, *ibid.*, p. 23.
[14] Wallace to Romero, Crawfordville, Indiana, April 12, 1867, *ibid.*, p. 157.
[15] Romero to Seward, Washington, April 20, 1867, *ibid.*, p. 5.
[16] Sturm, 1869: pp. 9–10.
[17] Wallace to Romero, New York, August 31, 1885, U.S. Congress, *House Exec. Doc. 33*, p. 48.
[18] Jonathan Tifft [of Corlies Co.] to Romero, New York, April 16, 1867, *ibid.*, p. 149.

action against the company or its secretary. Their reasoning was that such scandal would harm the Mexican cause and discredit other Mexican bonds that were about to be legitimately issued. It was also believed that Woodhouse would not cause any further trouble but would remain quiet out of gratitude that extreme measures were not pursued. Nevertheless, Woodhouse continued to harass and embarrass the Mexican government in its financial dealings, and he actually sold some spurious Mexican bonds represented to be those issued under his contract with Carvajal. As a final audacious action, in 1867 Woodhouse requested the United States Congress to confirm his contract and guarantee his right to issue Mexican bonds. His petition was referred to the House Committee on Foreign Affairs and was never reported out of that committee.[19]

When it became apparent that the Woodhouse contract could not be fulfilled, arrangements were made for a reputable financial house to take over the $30,000,000 Mexican bond issue. General Sturm had previously negotiated arms contracts through the firm of Corlies and Company, and he introduced Jonathan Tifft, a partner of Corlies, to Carvajal and Wallace. After several interviews Tifft was made the financial agent of the Mexican republic and a new contract was signed which had the approval of Romero.[20] The Mexican government sent orders to Carvajal that he should act in concert with the ambassador and insisted that Romero approve any contract or negotiations made by the commissioner.

The Carvajal-Corlies contract was drawn up by Wallace and signed by the contracting parties on September 11, 1865. It contained no concessions for railroads, telegraphs, or colonization plans, but it did grant the company 440,000 acres of agricultural land and about 2,500 acres of mining land. The financial firm agreed to put General Carvajal's bonds on the market and turn over the receipts from sales to him. The bonds were not to be sold at less than sixty cents on the dollar, and the company was to receive a commission on the sales as well as reimbursement for the costs of printing and putting the securities on the market.[21]

Although the company established a Mexican financial office in New York and engaged a full-time propaganda writer, the sale of bonds was a notable failure. In the year and a half before the bond issue terminated only $9,000 worth of bonds were sold for cash. The credit of the Republic of Mexico was indeed low, and the financial agents were unable to secure a guarantee of the bonds by the United States government which would have insured successful marketing. General Sturm reported that a Mexican officer who was in exile in New York and destitute for food and shelter "was refused even a loaf of bread for $1,000 in Mexican bonds."[22]

Herman Sturm, the purchasing agent hired by Carvajal, promoted a practical solution to the Mexican bond issue. He convinced American munitions manufacturers that the Juárez government would be successful in regaining control of Mexico and that the bonds were a valuable promise to pay. Thus he used the bonds to pay for ships, arms, and military stores, negotiating almost $2,000,000 in bonds in less than one year. Romero, in reporting on the use of bonds for munitions, stated that "at a cost of an obligation almost insignificant for Mexico, tremendous material assistance was obtained."[23]

General Carvajal went back to Mexico in the spring of 1866 leaving behind his agent, Jesús Fuentes y Muñoz, who had authority to sign the bonds. Sturm remained in New York buying and shipping military stores, while General Wallace was working in the Midwest and the East trying to organize an American volunteer corps. Romero had selected Carvajal as the man who could resolve the quarrels among the republican factions in the Matamoros region. Carvajal agreed to return to his homeland, and he ordered Sturm to send a shipload of arms to the area. He also expected to be reinforced by American volunteers under General Lew Wallace who were to assemble on the Rio Grande near Brownsville, Texas. Carvajal left Washington about the middle of May, was in New Orleans on the twenty-ninth, and began operations in his homeland the first part of June, 1866.

General Sheridan, headquartered in New Orleans, saw Carvajal when the latter visited him en route to Mexico. In his memoirs he observed that the Mexican general did not impress him favorably. Sheridan wrote, "He was old and cranky, yet, as he seemed anxious to do his best, I sent him over to Brownsville with credentials authorizing him to cross over into Mexico, and I followed him on the next boat."[24]

Carvajal quickly gathered an army and began operations to liberate the towns along the Rio Grande. By mid-June most of the towns except Matamoros had fallen to the republican forces. Carvajal was preparing to assault that port city when the imperial commander, Tomás Mejía, opened negotiations for a surrender; he offered to evacuate the city provided he could take his 500 men to the other side of the river and embark for points south. United States merchants of Matamoros prevailed upon Carvajal to grant the favorable terms, according to historian Hubert Howe Bancroft, who notes that on June 23, 1866, "the American flag was actually hoisted to protect the embarkation of Mejía."[25]

---

[19] Frazer, "The United States," 1944: p. 39.
[20] Sturm, 1869: p. 18.
[21] Carvajal-Corlies contract in Mexico, Legación, *Contratos*, 1868; pp. 443-447.
[22] Sturm to Romero, New York, August 28, 1866, in Sturm, 1872: p. 228; account of bonds negotiated by Sturm in Mexico, Legación, *Circulares*, 1868: **1**: pp. 463-468.
[23] Mexico, Legación, *Circulares*, 1868: **1**: pp. 462-463.
[24] Sheridan, 1902: **2**: pp. 219-220.
[25] Bancroft, 1888: **6**: pp. 252-253, note 47.

This "soft peace" eventually cost Carvajal his commission from the Juárez government and spelled the end of his public career. In the first place he should have referred Mejía's capitulation offer to his superior, General Escobedo, who had an army of 5,000 men near Matamoros. This army, which included hundreds of volunteers from the United States,[26] had recently won a decisive victory against the imperialists at Santa Gertrudis near Camargo, Tamaulipas, on June 16, and there is no reason to doubt that they could have easily overwhelmed Matamoros. By allowing one of the ablest of the imperialist generals to escape it meant that Mejía would be free to fight the Juarists again. But Carvajal no doubt had future provincial political plans in mind when he placated the merchants of the principal town of Tamaulipas by permitting the bloodless capitulation of June 23.

Carvajal took command of Matamoros planning to assemble a large military force within the city. But he soon alienated the sympathy of the residents by what one historian called "the violence of his character, by his lack of administrative tact, and because of his devotion to Americans of the United States."[27] Meanwhile, sailing from New York in July, the steamer *J.W. Everman*, loaded with military supplies, headed for Matamoros with General Wallace and other officers aboard. Arrival of the steamer at the Rio Grande port coincided with a local uprising against Carvajal, and the Mexican general barely escaped into Texas. In fact, one of the *Everman* passengers, Wilbur Stocking, reported in a letter to General Sturm that Carvajal killed the officer who tried to arrest him. Stocking also noted that the Americans were arrested and in much personal danger for some time but eventually they were permitted to cross over to Brownsville, Texas.[28]

A substantial portion of the *Everman* cargo was salvaged through the efforts of Wallace, Stocking, and Louis Avery, American vice-consul at Matamoros. The Americans claimed that the munitions were the personal property of United States citizens and subject to protection thereby. Stocking had three interviews with the new chief of Matamoros, Servando Canales, who finally permitted the goods to be transferred to Brownsville. Some of the medical stores and a large part of the arms and equipment had disappeared and were never recovered by the American agents; material lost through looting included 29 Enfield rifles, 155 revolvers, 750 sabers, 11,000 cartridges, 12,000 primers, 29 tarpaulins and 6 hospital tents. Wallace and Stocking ultimately disposed of the salvaged munitions by selling them to various Mexican field commanders.[29]

Meanwhile, Carvajal went into exile in Texas. Even before the August revolt his political future had been curtailed by action of the Juárez cabinet. In an order dated at Chihuahua August 4, 1866, Carvajal was accused of having negotiated with the traitor, Tomás Mejía, and of helping him and his command escape with the honors of war. Two days later Carvajal was formally relieved of his commission, and Santiago Tapia was named by Juárez as the new governor of Tamaulipas.[30] However, for some months Tapia was ignored by Canales in Matomoros and by Carvajal in Texas. The Matamoros debacle was further complicated by the fact that Canales was one of those who recognized Jesús González Ortega rather than Juárez as president of Mexico. Therefore Juaristas under General Escobedo besieged the port city until the end of November. At that time, after what historian Hubert Howe Bancroft called "the somewhat suspicious intervention of United States troops," Escobedo regained Matamoros and incorporated Canales's troops into his own army.[31]

Although Canales was politically rehabilitated, General Carvajal suffered the ignominious fate of another Mexican secret agent, General Plácido Vega. Both of these commissioners had a great admiration for the people of the United States, and both suffered the misfortune of having elements of their North American troops rebel against them. Both were also out of favor with their government when they returned from their secret missions in the United States. After a long exile in Texas, José María Carvajal returned to his home in Soto la Marina, Tamaulipas, where he died on August 19, 1874.[32]

General Carvajal's contribution to the republican cause during the French intervention lies more in the authority with which he was clothed than in his personal efforts and accomplishments. Powers granted him by the Juárez cabinet were greater than those given to any of the other secret agents in this period, and using those powers, his associates tried to aid Mexico. Although the 10,000 man auxiliary corps never materialized, some soldiers were enlisted in the United States for Mexican service as a result of the plans and recruitment activities of Carvajal and Wallace. The Mexican bond issue and its attendant propaganda campaign favoring the Juárez administration were an outgrowth of Carvajal's broad powers. So were shipments of arms to Mexico negotiated by Herman Sturm who was commissioned by Carvajal as purchasing agent for the neighboring nation. General Sturm's successful activities will be considered next.

---

[26] A French historian says there were 1,200 to 1,500 Americans in Escobedo's army, see Niox, 1874: p. 577.

[27] Arias, 1867: p. 79.

[28] Stocking to Sturm, Brownsville, August 13, 1866, in Sturm, 1872: pp. 39–40.

[29] Sturm, 1872: pp. 37–38, 54–55; Mexico, Legación, *Circulares*, 1868: **1**: pp. 475–476.

[30] Arias, 1867: p. 80; U.S. Congress, *House Exec. Doc. 1*, pt. 1: p. 413.

[31] Bancroft, 1888: **6**: p. 255, note 56. Details of United States intervention in Matamoros summarized in Blumberg, 1971: p. 113.

[32] *Expediente* XI/III/1-38, fol. 192, ADN.

IX. GENERAL STURM—ORDNANCE EXPEDITER

Considering the quantity of military supplies forwarded to Mexico, undoubtedly the most effective of the Mexican secret agents in the United States during the 1860's was General Herman Sturm. His efforts were all the more important because of his ability to buy military equipment on the paper-thin credit of the republican government of Mexico. After all, the intervention war was brought on by that government's lack of ability to honor its bonds or pay its foreign obligations. At the time of Sturm's employment the Juárez government, having lost control of most of the republic, held only a small enclave on the Rio Grande border, and it was questionable whether that administration would ever again rule from Mexico City. But Herman Sturm, who was personally wealthy and possessed invaluable contacts in the business, financial, and munitions circles of the United States, was able to buy about two million dollars worth of military hardware in exchange for the Juárez government's future promise to pay.[1]

Who was Herman W. Sturm—and how did he get involved in Mexico's troubles? Born in Hanover, Germany, in 1830, he immigrated to the United States some time before 1860. When the Civil War broke out he was living in Indiana, and because he had learned the munitions business abroad, Governor Oliver P. Morton commissioned him to set up an arms factory in Indianapolis. According to a history of that city, "quarters were rented on the square just south of the State House. . . . Captain Sturm selected men whom he instructed in the various processes of molding, swedging and perfecting bullets and cartridges, of filling shells and fashioning fuses."[2] By the end of the war Sturm was a general and chief of ordnance for the state of Indiana.

As a manufacturer, procurer, and expediter of military supplies, Sturm had notable success. At the same time he made valuable contacts with American munitions firms like Remington and du Pont as well as with several New York financial houses. According to General Wallace, Sturm's value to the Mexican cause was enhanced by the fact that he was "possessed of money in his own right, and that he could command more from members of his family and friends."[3]

As mentioned in chapter VII, Sturm got involved with the war in Mexico through his Hoosier friend Lew Wallace. It was General Wallace who suggested to representatives of the Mexican republican government that they should engage Sturm as an ordnance expediter. Wallace testified that Sturm was "an honorable man, and expert in arms and munitions of war, full of experience in their purchase, and especially favored with a general acquaintance with the business men of New York. . . ."[4] At a conference arranged by Wallace, Sturm was introduced to General José María Carvajal who had come to the United States seeking arms, men, and supplies for Mexico. Carvajal explained his mission to Sturm and tried to enlist him as a confidential purchasing agent, noting that the Juárez government wanted an American auxiliary force of 10,000 armed men who would be willing to emigrate to Mexico as soldier-colonists. The men were to assemble somewhere on the Rio Grande and be under the command of General Wallace. Sturm was offered a commission to provide all the munitions and supplies for this army corps as well as Mexican troops that would be added to the force. The table of organization for this army called for 40,000 infantry, 3,000 cavalry, 2,000 engineers, and 15 artillery batteries. General Carvajal was optimistic;

FIG. 9. General Herman Sturm, ordnance expediter and Mexican secret agent. Photo courtesy of the Indiana State Library.

---

[1] A preliminary version of this chapter appeared in the *Indiana Magazine of History* **58**: pp. 1–15.

[2] Nolan, 1943: p. 139. McKee, 1947: p. 96, says he was a colonel, but Sturm, 1869: pp. 3–4, reprints a contract signed by Sturm as brigadier general and chief of ordnance. Genealogical information in letters from a niece of Sturm, Miss Helen Loeper, to the author, April 6 and June 10, 1959.

[3] Wallace, 1906: **2**: p. 863.

[4] *Ibid.*

he thought that within three months the 10,000 Americans and required munitons could be on Mexican soil.[5]

Sturm signed a contract with Carvajal on May 1, 1865, accepting a commission as "Agent of the Mexican Republic, for the purchase and shipment of all material necessary for the prosecution of the war against the French; also as Secret Agent to raise and transport emigrants from the United States to Mexico." For his services Sturm was to receive from $10,000 to $20,000 as well as a brigadier general's commission in the Mexican army on the termination of the Civil War in the United States. Sturm was also authorized to hire officers to assist him and to promise them, if they emigrated to Mexico, positions and salaries equivalent to those last held by them in the United States. Carvajal pledged himself to place at Sturm's disposal all the funds necessary for the fulfillment of contracts for arms and emigrants as well as a secret service fund, "to be used at his discretion, to gain sympathy, opinion and action in behalf of the Republic of Mexico in the United States."[6]

The two generals signed another document which was a power of authority Sturm could use in his negotiations; the paper was back-dated March 1, 1865, and place of execution given as Soto la Marina, Mexico. The object of this ruse was to avoid any difficulty or embarrassment that might result if such a document signed in the United States came into the hands of an enemy of the Mexican republic. The power of authority was signed by Juan N. Navarro, consul-general of the Mexican constitutional government, and by Matías Romero, Mexican minister to the United States. Romero certified that Carvajal was governor of Tamaulipas, Mexico, and that the general was authorized by the Juárez government to make contracts for purchase of arms. He added that "any contract or purchase that he will make in pursuance of and in accordance to said instructions will bind the National Government of Mexico and the faith of the country."[7]

Within the terms of his secret commission Sturm immediately began to execute the obligations of the agreement. He visited arms manufacturers in Cincinnati, Cleveland, Louisville, Indianapolis, New York, Boston, Pittsburgh, St. Louis, and other centers where military equipment was made and contracted for war stores. He also hired some agents and sent them to various parts of the country and made arrangements for transporting emigrants to Mexico via the Mississippi River and Texas. For the expedition to Mexico he enlisted several former United States Army officers who had been mustered out before the official close of the Civil War.[8]

In the first part of August, 1865, Sturm and Carvajal met in New York to discuss financing of the arms and emigrant contracts. The Mexican general had already contracted with the United States, European and West Virginia Land and Mining Company to negotiate a loan of $30,000,000, predicated on bonds of the Mexican republic. Carvajal gave Sturm two drafts on the company, one for $20,000 in Mexican bonds to defray certain printing and advertising costs, and another order for $1,500,000 in currency as reimbursement for money advanced and obligations due. At the same time Sturm was assured that within a few days he would be given another sum of money that would enable him to settle all the contracts he had signed. But it soon developed that the land and mining concern was a bubble corporation which Sturm characterized as "an unmitigated swindle—its resources fictitious—its pretenses a fraud."[9] The drafts were refused by the company secretary, and Sturm was forced to pacify his creditors, placate emigrants, and cancel contracts for war stores.

About this time the resources of the Mexican republican government had reached their nadir. As one Mexican general put it, "our enemy is the most powerful in the world, and actually holds our cities and the forts from which we chiefly derive our revenue; and the head of our Government, with his Cabinet, is in the corner of the most distant state of the Republic, without money, or credit, or army. . . ."[10] Official Mexican missions in the United States also suffered from lack of cash and credit; Sturm discovered that the Mexican legation in Washington was so pressed for funds that it could barely meet its necessary expenses. Furthermore, General Carvajal had signed up a number of former Union officers whose hotel bills and other expenses had mounted to a large debt, and owing to the failure of the bond issue, Carvajal could not meet this obligation. To avoid disgrace and failure of future plans it was absolutely necessary that the facts about Mexico's bankrupt condition be kept from the public.

Like so many failing causes this one needed an injection of cash to forestall complete collapse. So Sturm, to salvage his investment of time and money, advanced General Carvajal about $4,600 which was used to mollify the contract cancellations. As a reward for his extraordinary services and as an additional incentive, Carvajal, on behalf of the Mexican government, gave a land grant to Herman Sturm and his brothers Robert and Frederick, who had worked with him. The patent, dated September 21, 1865, was for 50 acres of mining land and one square league (4,439 acres) of agricultural land in the states of Tamaulipas or San Luis Potosí.[11] Rescue from the bond fiasco was more difficult, but through Sturm's contacts in the financial

---

[5] Sturm, 1869: p. 2.
[6] *Ibid.*, pp. 3–4.
[7] *Ibid.*, pp. 6–7.
[8] McKee, 1947: p. 96; Sturm, 1869: p. 8.

[9] Sturm, 1869: p. 9.
[10] Carvajal to Sturm, New York, August 25, 1865, in Sturm, 1869: p. 14.
[11] Sturm, 1872: pp. vi, vii; Sturm, 1869: p. 19.

world, the reputable New York firm of Corlies and Company was engaged to take over the bond issue.[12]

In conjunction with the new bond issue a propaganda campaign was waged to reinforce American public opinion about the Juárez government and its prospects for success. General Carvajal, in a letter of secret instructions, told Sturm that "the sympathy, voice and influence of the most prominent men in the country must be gained; the Press must be on our side; above all we must enlist in the cause the most active and untiring agents, *and if they should at the same time be agents of the United States Government, so much the better.*" Then Carvajal pledged $500,000 in U. S. currency, or its equivalent in Mexican bonds, to be used by Sturm as a secret service fund. Furthermore, Sturm was not to be held responsible for divulging names of those who aided Mexico and received money from this fund.[13]

As an assistant in the propaganda war, Sturm engaged the services of the Hoosier social reformer Robert Dale Owen. Both men had previously been commissioned by the Indiana governor to procure military supplies for the state troops; now they would work together to publicize the predicament and potential of the Mexican republic.[14] Owen's specific task was related to the projected bond issue—confidence in Juárez and the success of his campaign had to be fortified to insure a successful marketing of the securities. From material and dispatches supplied by the Mexican legation he wrote newspaper articles that glorified Juárez's victories, republican institutions, the Monroe Doctrine, and economic resources of Mexico. At the same time, the Maximilian regime was excoriated owing to its monarchical nature and because it was imposed and supported by foreign bayonets. Other phases of Owen's activities in behalf of Mexico included public speaking and private influence peddling. Along with Herman Sturm he attended the gala New York opening of the Mexican Financial Agency on November 2, 1865, and Owen's biographer notes that "surrounded by swarthy diplomats and comic opera generals, he spoke briefly on the danger inherent in an empire to the south."[15] Robert Dale Owen also had at least three interviews with President Johnson trying to get some official American support for the Mexican loan, or at least a statement that Maximilian would never be recognized by the United States. When bond sales lagged, he tried, unsuccessfully, to get the Philadelphia banker Jay Cooke interested in the loan. In an attempt to have the United States government guarantee the bond issue Owen drafted a proposed bill, lobbied in Washington, and testified before the House Committee on Foreign Affairs.[16]

In 1866 Owen wrote six pamphlets in support of the Juárez government which were published anonymously, the printing cost borne by General Sturm. The first pamphlet called for the United States government to guarantee a loan of fifty million dollars to Mexico. Appealing to patriotism it asked, "shall we scruple and hestitate to put forth . . . a modicum of pecuniary aid to an outraged people, our next neighbors, so that they, not we, may maintain this war for their independence; may right themselves by their own efforts, and succeed, as we succeeded against another foreign monarch, eighty years ago, at Saratoga and at Yorktown?"[17] Of course these panegyric publications presented a biased view of events in Mexico, but that was their function. Although public sale of Mexican bonds was a failure, the propaganda effort was effective in gaining sympathy for the Juárez cause. Many Americans wanted to see the republican government restored to full power in Mexico, but at the same time they hesitated to invest in securities of that country. As bond sales declined and the Mexican war drew to a close, Robert Dale Owen severed his connection with the Mexican enterprise.

Meanwhile, General Sturm found the answer to Mexico's financial troubles. His expedient was to trade the bonds for war goods, and he persuaded a number of American arms companies to take the bonds as payment for purchases of ships, guns, powder, grenades, uniforms, medical supplies, and other military stores. Of course the bonds were discounted and negotiated at sixty per cent of their face value, but the important thing was that Mexico's credit was at last accepted. The Mexican minister was nonplused but enthusiastic about this development, and he properly credited Sturm with solving the difficult logistic and financial problem facing Mexican secret agents in the United States. In commenting on Sturm's triumph, General Wallace noted, "Here his experience, skill, knowledge of dealers and prices, his tirelessness and loyalty were successful."[18] One should not overlook the fact that American munitions makers had a large inventory on their hands at this time, only a few months after the end of the Civil War; undoubtedly they were glad to unload their surplus even though payment was in Mexican bonds.

Sturm dispatched his first large shipment of munitions to Matamoros, Mexico, on July 16, 1866, aboard the steamer *J.W. Everman* with General Wallace heading the list of passengers. The well-publicized embarkation served to refute the claim that the Mexican republic had ceased to exist. A small steamer loaded with well-wishers, newspaper reporters, and a brass band accompanied the ship out to sea, and Sturm noted that

---

[12] Sturm, 1869: p. 18.
[13] *Ibid.*, pp. 14–16.
[14] Owen placed arms contracts in Europe, 1861–1863, Leopold, 1940: pp. 373, 375.
[15] *Ibid.*, p. 374.
[16] *Ibid.;* Sturm, 1872: p. xii.

[17] Pamphlets listed with Owen's writings, Leopold, 1940: p. 424.
[18] Wallace, 1906: **2**: p. 864; Romero's evaluation in Mexico, Legación, *Responsabilidades,* 1867: p. 13.

he provided "collation" to cheer the voyagers on their way.[19] The cargo of military hardware included 5,020 Enfield rifles, 1,000 pistols, 618,000 cartridges, 1,100,000 percussion caps, 5,000 pounds of gunpowder, 1,000 cavalry swords, 6 artillery pieces with 20,400 rounds of ammunition, 3,000 mess kits, 13,801 knapsacks, 1,308 pairs of underdrawers, 813 frying pans, and a large quantity of medical and surgical equipment including surgical and dental instruments, assorted medicines, and 6 hospital tents.[20]

As noted in the previous chapter the supplies on the *Everman* were consigned to General Carvajal, who had returned to Mexico and regained control of the port of Matamoros. But a local revolt against Carvajal forced him into exile on the very day that the cargo and men of the *Everman* arrived in Matamoros. Wallace and his group were briefly jailed, and it was some time before the war stores could be salvaged and warehoused. In the meantime, looting had reduced the cargo considerably. Wallace and one of Sturm's agents eventually disposed of most of the rescued war stores by arranging sales with representatives of individual Mexican field commanders.[21]

Another fiasco involved the gunboat *Sheridan* which Sturm purchased for $231,333 in bonds and sent to Mexico in the summer of 1866. The cannon and munitions for the gunboat were embarked on another vessel because, according to Sturm, "it would have been impolitic and almost impossible in that time to send this boat from here with its armament."[22] The ship carrying the *Sheridan's* guns later foundered in a storm and sank in the Atlantic Ocean; thus the Mexicans acquired an impotent gunboat. More than a year later the *Sheridan* was armed and sent to blockade the port of Veracruz, but bad luck prevailed again and the gunboat sank off the coast of Tamaulipas.[23]

The revolt in Matamoros and the difficulties with the gunboat delayed Sturm's activities for some months, but eventually he was again able to negotiate Mexican bonds for war stores. Following Carvajal's defeat and exile to Texas the Mexican government advised Sturm that he should no longer take orders from that general; henceforth he was to work directly under Minister Romero, who would have to approve any future contracts. Romero gave Sturm some new instructions regarding the type of goods to buy, the wording of contracts, and the use of bonds. One of the provisions stated that nothing was to be purchased that could not be transported to Mexico. This clause was no doubt inserted because another secret agent had purchased a rifle factory, brick building and all, and the Mexican government was embarrassed over this act.[24] Sturm was ordered not to buy any more ships and advised not to send any food supplies since the basis for feeding Mexican soldiers was Indian corn, which was plentiful in Mexico. Another section of the instructions warned against purchasing "articles which may be considered necessary for the United States army, which would be as articles of luxury for our army—such as camp tents, shoes, stockings, coffee, etc."[25]

Acting under the terms of his new instructions, on November 11, 1866, Sturm sent the ship *Vixen* with a cargo of war goods to Minatitlán, Veracruz. General Sturm's oldest brother, Robert C. Sturm, went along as supercargo, and another brother, Captain Frederick C. Sturm, went with this ship to aid Mexico in the artillery service. Two Mexican commissioners, General Pedro de Baranda and Señor Justo Benítez, also accompanied this shipment of arms consigned to the Mexican army under General Porfirio Díaz. The cargo included 5,100 rifles, 50 Remington pistols, 117,056 rounds of ammunition, 334,500 percussion caps, 616 cavalry swords, 2 telescopes, 12 copies of Hammond's hygiene book, and a large amount of medical and surgical equipment. The military stores went directly into the hands of General Porfirio Díaz and his second in command, Alejandro García, and were used by General Díaz in his recapture of Puebla.[26]

Later in the same month the *Suwanee* was loaded with military supplies expedited by General Sturm. This vessel put to sea on November 27, 1866, with a Mexican officer, Governor Juan José Baz of Michoacán, in charge of the cargo, but on December 4 the ship foundered in a storm and sank off the Carolina coast, the passengers barely escaping with their lives. The cargo had not been insured because Sturm had received no instructions to do so, and as he later stated, the regulations of the United States Army which had been given him as a guide prohibited military officers from insuring government property. Lost in the shipwreck were 20 army wagons, 2 rifled cannon for the gunboat *Sheridan,* 1 ten-pound cannon, 5,000 Enfield rifles, 2,900 repeating carbines, 1,500,000 percussion caps, 1,200 wad hooks and rifle swabs, 13,750 pounds of powder, 458 grenades, 1,340 boxes of grapeshot, 751 cavalry swords and scabbards, 75 pairs of spurs, 2 telescopes, 6,409 knapsacks, and other items of assorted field and medical equipment. When the Mexican minister heard about the mishap, he wrote Sturm, "This disagreeable incident has decided me to stop all further purchases of goods for the Mexican government. . . . What is the use of our purchasing at high prices,

---

[19] Sturm, 1872: p. xiv.
[20] Cargo itemized in tables 3 and 4.
[21] Wallace, 1906: 2: pp. 875–876: Mexico, Legación, *Circulares,* 1868: 1: pp. 475–476.
[22] Sturm, 1872: p. 324.
[23] *Ibid.,* p. 210.

[24] Romero's instructions in Sturm, 1869: pp. 39–41. Data on other agent in Part II, box 1, fol. 204, Enrique Antonio Mejía Papers, Bancroft Library.
[25] Sturm, 1869: p. 41.
[26] *Ibid.,* p. 60; Mexico, Legación, *Responsabilidades,* 1867: p. 14; Mexico, Legación, *Circulares,* 1868: 1: p. 477.

TABLE 3
Ordnance Supplies Shipped to Mexico by General Sturm
Adapted from data in México, Legación, United States, *Circulares y Otras Publicaciones* (Mexico, 1868) 1: 475–486

Items	Total	7/16/1866 J. W. Everman	11/11/66 Vixen	11/27/66 Suwanee	3/3/67 Gen. McCallum*	5/18/67 Veto	8/1867 Zingarella	8/1867 Samuel F. Keese
Rifles, carbines	20,020	5,020	5,100	7,900	200	500	1,300	
Pistols	1,055	1,000	53	2				
Pistol cases	342	340		2				
Cartridges	1,044,520	618,000	117,056	109,464	20,000	50,000		130,000
Friction primers	30,000	30,000						
Percussion caps	2,934,500	1,100,000	334,500	1,500,000				
Bullet pouches	1,750		1,750					
Bullet molds	21			21				
Rifle slings	4,600		1,500	3,100				
Cartridge belts	17,000	6,000	3,500	5,000	200	500	1,800	
Wad hooks	1,200			1,200				
Bayonet sheaths	5,000	5,000						
Rifle swabs	3,200		2,000	1,200				
Artillery pieces	6	6						
Cannon	3			3				
Art. shells, boxes	20,400	20,400						
Hinges for above	816	816						
Fuses, feet	800		800					
Gunpowder, lbs.	57,500	5,000	6,250	13,750	2,000	5,000	25,500	
Grapeshot, boxes	1,340			1,340				
Grenades	458			458				
Swords	5,874	1,000	616	751	200	400	2,907	
Sword belts	5,531	1,000	300	731	200	400	2,900	
Cavalry equip.	250						250	
Pack saddles	12		12					
Spurs	75			75				
Field glasses	4		2	2				
Telescopes	4		2	2				
Tarpaulins	45	45						
Torpedo boat	1						1	

* Sturm's private cargo of arms not included.

needed articles, if we can not get them to Mexico?"[27] As far as the republic of Mexico was concerned this disaster was more important from the logistic than the financial standpoint.

Juarist armies had a critical shortage of guns and ammunition at this turning point in the war, and the lack of munitions became more pronounced as they began to assault and lay seige to the cities of Veracruz, Querétaro, and Mexico City. To meet this increased demand for munitions, especially artillery powder and shells, General Sturm fitted out additional ships with military supplies and sent them to Mexico. The *General McCallum* sailed for Tampico on March 3, 1867, carrying arms to General Pavón, military commandant in that area. The bulk of the cargo was made up of a private shipment of arms, the property of General Sturm. The Mexican minister had agreed to permit this speculative venture, especially since field commanders had been sending special commissioners to the United States with lists of needed arms. About this time Romero received official word from his government to make no more arms contracts on behalf of the supreme government but permitting negotiations with individual commanders. Aboard the *General McCallum* for sale in Mexico were 5,000 rifles, 1,100 boxes of carbines and assorted rifles, 1,000 revolvers, 730,000 cartridges, 8,000 percussion caps, 7,000 pounds of gunpowder, and other boxes of swords, muskets, pistols, and ammunition. Two of Sturm's agents, Robert C. Sturm and Wilbur F. Stocking, went along to manage the sale of the merchandise.[28]

The fate of the *McCallum* resembled that of the ill-fated *Everman* expedition to Matamoros. Arrival of Sturm's cargo at Tampico on April 15, 1867, coincided with a local revolt, and the military stores were seized and interned in a public warehouse. Although Robert Sturm remained in Tampico for some time trying to retrieve or sell the arms, he was apparently unsuccessful in liberating any goods or money. Moreover, he contracted some kind of tropical fever that took many months to cure.

In spite of the difficulties encountered, Herman Sturm

---

[27] Sturm, 1872: p. 117; Mexico, Legación, *Circulares*, 1868: 1: pp. 479–482; see tables 3 and 4.

[28] Sturm, 1872: pp. 123–133; Mexico, Legación, *Circulares*, 1868: 1: p. 483; NA/RG 76, doc. 762.

TABLE 4

Quartermaster and Medical Supplies Shipped to Mexico by General Sturm

Adapted from data in México, Legación, United States, *Circulares y Otras Publicaciones*, (México, 1868) 1: pp. 475–486

Items	Total	J. W. Everman	Vixen	Suwanee	Gen. McCallum	Veto	Zingarella	Samuel F. Reese
Infantry caps	1,119	1,119						
Infantry coats	6,265					1,061	5,204	
Covers for caps	5,000	5,000						
Belts	5,200	5,200						
Braids, yards	2,910			2,910				
Gloves, officers	48			48				
Jackets, leather	500			500				
Underdrawers	1,308	1,308						
Knapsacks	46,210	13,801		6,409		2,000	10,000	14,000
Canteens	274			274				
Mess kits	3,000	3,000						
Frying pans	813	813						
Tents	518	6		12	50	100	350	
Army wagons	30	10		20				
Field cot	1			1				
Field basket	1			1				
Field desk	1			1				
Corkscrew	1			1				
Knife set	1			1				
Straps	1			1				
Spring dagger	1			1				
Dental instr.	13	5	8					
Surgery instr.	31	13	18					
Syringes	12		12					
Hygiene books	12		12					
Medicines, box	26	9	3		14			
Sets of tablets	17		17					
Surgery sponges	12	12						
Scarificators	10		10					
Tourniquets	5		5					

made four more arms shipments to Mexico in 1867. On May 18 the *Veto* sailed for Matamoros, consigned to General Berriozábal, commandant at that port. The usual assortment of carbines, ammunition, swords, and quartermaster equipment made up the cargo manifest. The following August the bark *Zingarella* and the schooner *Samuel F. Keese* were sent with military stores to General Porfirio Díaz. In October the *Keese* was again dispatched to Mexico, but like the *Suwanee* was lost at sea. In addition to guns and ammunition the *Zingarella* transported an unusual item to Mexico, a one-man torpedo boat. This unique weapon, built of iron, was about 30 feet long and was powered by an oil-burning engine which was supposed to be virtually noiseless. The torpedo boat had a cruising speed of 5 knots and a range of 25 to 30 miles. It carried a torpedo on an outrigger 20 feet from the bow, and in combat the boat was to run up to the target, the torpedo would explode on contact, and the boat would return for a reload.[29] Tables 3 and 4 indicate the variety and quantity of ordnance and quartermaster supplies sent to Mexico by Sturm.

The intervention war finally ended about the time the torpedo boat and the other supplies aboard the *Zingarella* arrived in Mexico. General Sturm totaled up his account books, made itemized statements of his purchases and of his disposition of the Mexican bonds, and forwarded these along with a letter detailing his services on behalf of Mexico to the Mexican minister in Washington. He mentioned that he expected to be compensated for his two years of labor and reimbursed for his personal expenditures in accordance with the agreements signed with General Carvajal. In the letter Sturm referred by name to all his agents and employees, giving their dates of service, and he noted that the men "remained at their posts and cooperated valiantly and enthusiastically even though they were very frequently embarrassed by the fact that their salaries were not paid at the stipulated time." [30]

But General Sturm was to have a prolonged ordeal with the Mexican government before he received any remuneration. He made two trips to Mexico City in this connection in 1867 and 1868 and managed to get

---

[29] Cargoes of these ships in Mexico, Legación, *Circulares*, 1868: **1**, p. 483; loss of *Keese* in Sturm, 1872: p. 250. The torpedo boat purchased for $7,500 form George M. Ramsey of New York; its description in NA/RG 76, doc. 764.

[30] Letter of August 23, 1867, in Sturm, 1872: pp. 319–328.

$43,500 which he accepted as payment on account but which the government considered as payment in full. Sturm maintained that this amount represented only one-third of his personal expenditures not to mention the sum promised him or the land grants which he was to receive. Along with other creditors and holders of Mexican bonds he appealed to the United States-Mexican Claims Commission which sat in Washington from 1868 to 1876. But the commission turned down Sturm's claim for $670,000 saying that his agreement was with General Carvajal, not the Mexican government and, furthermore, that Carvajal had exceeded his powers in giving the grants and commission to Sturm.[31]

As late as 1888 Sturm was still attempting to collect from the Díaz administration in Mexico what he could not get from that of Juárez. By that time Sturm was living in Denver, Colorado, without sufficient funds to leave that city. An Indianapolis lawyer, William Henderson, to whom Sturm was in debt knew that the ex-general still had a valuable claim against the Mexican government, so he agreed to pay Sturm's expenses for a trip to Mexico hoping thereby to collect not only the old debt but 5 per cent of any new settlement.[32] Sturm went to Mexico City in 1888 and the following year he obtained a settlement of $210,854.50. The payment, however, was to be made in Mexican bonds which were worth only one-third their par value. By 1891 Sturm still had not received either the bonds or their cash equivalent, so he and his lawyer made another trip to the Mexican capital. Apparently this trip was successful, for later in the year Henderson sued Sturm claiming the latter had not lived up to the agreement regarding the lawyer's commission fee. Growing out of this wrangle was another litigation wherein the general sued the lawyer for defamation of character and damages, but both legal actions were cut short by Henderson's death in 1892. General Sturm lived on in Denver where he amassed a small fortune in mining enterprises before his death on October 17, 1906.[33]

Herman Sturm's contribution to the defense effort of the Mexican republic is best summed up in a letter from General Lew Wallace to President Díaz. Referring to an official report of Minister Romero acknowledging that six or seven armies of the republic were provisioned by Sturm, Wallace asked:

> How shall the value of such services be measured? By what standard, except the liberty of your people, not to speak of the life of republican Mexico? It would insult you to speak here as an accountant; time, energy, judgement, faithfulness, especially money advanced in aid of the cause he espoused, are items which cannot be tabulated and cast up. One thing I know, he impoverished himself, his family, and many of his friends in the work to which he dedicated himself.[34]

Considering the difficulties, disappointments, and disasters that General Sturm had to face during his confidential assignment, it is amazing that he persevered until the end of the intervention. Although adversity plagued his attempts to receive compensation for services rendered, Sturm continued to have faith in a final settlement. In the history of that period it is difficult to find a similar example of loyalty and friendship to the Mexican republic, especially by a noncitizen of that country.

X. THE RECKONING—ACCOMPLISHMENTS AND ROLE OF THE AGENTS

Maximilian's execution and the entry of Juárez into Mexico City in the summer of 1867 put a dramatic end to the war known as the French intervention. With the Juarist victory there was no longer a need for government agents to smuggle arms from abroad; indeed, considering the possibility of internal revolts there was a plethora of rifles in Mexico.

Reasons behind the triumph of the Mexican republicans and the concurrent downfall of the empire have been debated for years on both sides of the Atlantic. Most writers will agree that the Juaristas were impotent as long as thousands of French troops remained in Mexico. The crux of the problem then is why the French army was ordered home in 1866. From the European point of view there were two compelling reasons for the return of the Gauls. First, by 1865 there was considerable French discontent and disgust with their Mexican venture. Intellectuals protested, so did members of the Chamber of Deputies, and French daily newspapers record numerous public demonstrations against the costly Mexican expedition. The rise of Prussia, evidenced by easy victories over Denmark in 1864 and Austria in 1866, was a trenchant stimulus for Napoleon III to recall his expeditionary forces. Even if they were not actually required to protect the homeland, the continued presence of soldiers and sailors abroad weakened the French military establishment on the continent.

Books written in the United States have usually emphasized Secretary of State William Seward's diplomacy and credited him with forcing Napoleon III to recall his army from Mexico. There was a distinct possibility of a Franco-American war in 1865, and talk of vindicating the Monroe Doctrine emanated from high places in the United States. Generals Grant, Sheridan, Banks, and Wright were among those who urged military action to enforce the Monroe Doctrine. But Seward outmaneuvered the military strategists by his Fabian tactics and by substituting diplomacy for armed threats

---

[31] Sturm, 1869: pp. 85, 88, 92; NA/RG 76, doc. 676; see also U.S. Congress, *Sen. Exec. Doc. 31*, pp. 54–55.

[32] Romero, 1892: pp. 16–17.

[33] *Ibid.*, pp. 8, 9, 11, 49, 54; Sturm's obituary in Denver, Colorado, *Post*, October 18, 1906.

[34] Wallace to Díaz, August 15, 1889, in Wallace, 1906: 2: p. 864.

or aggressive actions. His technique was never better demonstrated than when he diverted General Schofield from heading an American volunteer corps in Mexico by sending him on a junket to Paris. Although Seward's dispatches to France after the end of the Civil War became increasingly more antagonistic toward the French intervention in Mexico, it was also clear that he was not willing to risk war with France over the issue.

The situation in Mexico itself influenced decisions made in Europe. Maximilian was gradually weaned away from French advisers by his Mexican confidents until he was not even on speaking terms with Marshall Bazaine, commander of the French forces in Mexico. French troops, like any occupation army, naturally aroused the hostility of many Mexicans—republicans and imperalists. Other notes of discord and signs pointing toward the collapse of the Mexican empire included an empty treasury and constant strife among conservatives, clericals, and monarchists. Hastening decline of the empire was the growing strength of the constitutionalists beginning in 1866. Campaigns of Generals Escobedo, Díaz, Régules, and Corona were successful once they received modern weapons from across the border. Three of these generals also had United States army veterans servicing their artillery pieces and serving in their lines. The volunteers and munitions were sent to Mexico by the special commissioners of Juárez and his field commanders.

Plácido Vega was the first of the major secret agents sent to the United States by the Juárez government. He was also the only emissary who went north well supplied with funds and credit, but his resources evaporated when the French seized the customhouses of Mazatlán and Guaymas. Working against difficult odds, Vega managed to forward over 20,000 rifles and a substantial amount of ammunition to Mexico. He also recruited and sent several companies of American volunteers to join Mexican republican armies. The frustrations that he encountered during his mission to California more than once prompted him to quit, but he remained until he had accomplished some of the goals specified in his orders.

Operating on both the Atlantic and Pacific coasts, General Gaspar Sánchez Ochoa had bold plans for liberating his homeland. To pay for the ships and arms he expected to send to Mexico, the general issued ten million dollars worth of national bonds, but they were as valueless as Confederate money in the summer of 1865. Sánchez Ochoa had no difficulty in attracting adventurers and speculative knaves into the camp of the Mexican republicans, and he made all sorts of promises to these opportunists. His poor judgment of men and a reprimand from Juárez led him to support González Ortega in his fruitless bid for the presidency of Mexico. This was the greatest blunder of his ill-starred mission, and it resulted in his temporary incarceration in a Mexico City prison. The only tangible accomplishment of General Sánchez Ochoa's commission was his sponsoring of the Brannan contingent of volunteers, the group that formed the basis of the American Legion of Honor in Mexico.

Activities of Lew Wallace on behalf of the Mexican republic embraced organizing a corps of American volunteers for service in Mexico. This large paper army, like the one organized by Colonel Allen in the name of González Ortega, was never assembled due to a lack of funds. However, one of Wallace's men, Colonel Crawford, did recruit a small force of soldiers of fortune who moved across the Rio Grande and captured the city of Bagdad from the imperialists. This exploit was so mismanaged that the United States Army was forced to intervene, jailing Crawford and dispersing the volunteers. Wallace's second attempt to introduce American arms and volunteers into Mexico was the ill-fated *Everman* expedition which left him stranded in Mexico with a shipload of arms. Perhaps the greatest service Wallace rendered the Mexican republic was the assistance he gave General Carvajal during the latter's stay in New York. He not only paid his living expenses, but he also provided legal assistance for the Mexican agent and introduced him to several Americans who were prominent in financial and business circles.

President Juárez granted broader powers to General José Carvajal than to any other special commissioner sent to the United States, but in spite of his extended authorization Carvajal was later accused of exceeding his orders. This agent floated, or at least launched, a Mexican bond issue of $30,000,000 which was unsuccessful as far as raising money was concerned; however, several million dollars worth of the bonds were used to purchase needed military supplies. The Carvajal bonds were slowly redeemed by the Mexican government, the last of them being honored some twenty years after the date of issue. Carvajal's success as a military commander was short-lived when he returned to Mexico. Perhaps, like Plácido Vega and Sánchez Ochoa, he had remained abroad too long.

Herman Sturm became a secret agent of the Mexican republic through his connection with Wallace and Carvajal. Of the individual Mexican agents in the United States during the French intervention, all of whom were commissioned to purchase and convey war stores to the Juaristas, General Sturm was by far the most efficient and productive. Some of his shipments were thwarted, but military supplies he forwarded outfitted several republican armies and doubtless contributed to their victories in the closing years of the war. Like Wallace, Sturm used his own funds to cover personal expenses expecting reimbursement at the end of the war, and like all the other Yankees who were closely connected with the Mexican secret agents, he tried to get mining and railroad concessions in payment for his services. Of course the 1860's was a period of great railroad building and mining activity in the United

States, but Wallace and Sturm still thought of Mexico as a romantic land rich with gold and silver mines, and they wanted a small mine or two rather than payment in money.

Any reckoning of the work of Mexican agents in the United States would be incomplete without mention of Matías Romero, the great Mexican minister who served almost twenty-five years as his country's representative in Washington, D. C. In addition to his official capacity during the French intervention, Romero had confidential powers and functions that resembled those delegated to the special agents. But most important, Romero served as the one unifying factor and coordinator of activities of the various Mexican agents in the United States. His job was made difficult because of the relatively slow communications of that period, and because the men he was coordinating often refused to cooperate with each other or to inform him of their plans and accomplishments. Several of the commissioners thought their powers were equal to and independent of those of the Mexican minister. Nevertheless, Romero managed to oversee the major undertakings of the several confidential emissaries and to report their successes and failures to the Juárez cabinet.

In retrospect, the conduct of the Mexican secret agents who operated in the United States will bear extensive criticism, but the sum total of their efforts was significant. Although they engaged in propaganda efforts, recruited volunteers for the Mexican army, and floated national bonds, it was the material aid they forwarded that was a major contribution to the republican war effort. Military goods from the United States outfitted whole armies with the latest type of equipment; once that was accomplished, the Juaristas began to win battles and regain territory. Although events in Europe dictated the termination of the French intervention, the militant resurgence of the Mexican republicans would have been impossible without the aid secured by secret agents in the United States.

BIBLIOGRAPHY

Sources that document the story of United States aid to President Juárez of Mexico include the private papers of several key participants. The most important collection is the correspondence of Matías Romero, housed in the Banco de México. Although the archive contains more than one hundred thousand folios of original letters addressed to the Mexican minister, a published descriptive catalog which calendars the correspondence and provides an alphabetical index simplifies the researcher's task. All of the principal topics and personalities are covered; one can find details about arms contracts, bond negotiations, military recruitment, and activities of secret agents (see Monroy, 1965–1970).

Manuscript materials relating to two Mexican secret agents are in libraries in the United States. General Plácido Vega's papers at the Bancroft Library, University of California, consist of more than two thousand folios, most of them from the period when Vega was in California seeking arms for Juárez. In addition to letters, eight of them from Benito Juárez, there are receipts, customs declarations, hotel bills, Mexican government proclamations, telegrams, and contracts. The Lew Wallace Collection at the Indiana Historical Society has pertinent correspondence, financial accounts, legal papers relating to Mexico, photographs, and drawings.

Affidavits from American volunteers describing their service in Juárez's army are located in the United States National Archives. They are filed, along with supporting evidence such as military commissions, letters, photographs, and receipts, in the section entitled United States–Mexican Claims Commission of 1868–1876. That file also has sworn claims from Lew services to the Mexican Republic.
Wallace and Herman Sturm in which they detail their

Excellent printed documentation for this topic is found in four publications issued by the Mexican legation in Washington. The most important of these imprints is a ten-volume collection of the correspondence of Minister Romero (see Mexico, Legación, *Correspondencia*, 1870–1892). Of considerable value are two volumes reprinting public notices and reports issued by Romero (see Mexico, Legación, *Circulares*, 1868). A volume devoted to contracts negotiated by the secret agents was also published in Mexico (see Mexico, Legación, *Contratos*, 1868); and a summary of Mexican governmental obligations resulting from the contracts was issued (see Mexico, Legación, *Responsabilidades*, 1867).

The appended bibliography is a selected listing of the more important items consulted for this study. Those works dealing chiefly with Emperor Maximilian or the French intervention in Mexico, although basic to an understanding of the period, have not been included because they give little or no insight to the story of arms shipments across the border to the Juárez forces.

I. MANUSCRIPTS

Archives du Ministère des Affaires Etrangères, Paris, France
  Corresp. Politique des Consuls, Etats Unis, Charles de Cazotte
Archivo Histórico Militar, Sec. de la Defensa Nacional, México, D.F.
  General Plácido Vega, personnel *expediente*
  General José María J. Carvajal, personnel *expediente*
Banco de México, Mexico, D.F.
  Archivo Histórico de Matías Romero (AHMR)
Bancroft Library, University of California, Berkeley, California
  Jesús González Ortega Papers
  Alfred A. Green, MS "Life and Adventures of a '47er"
  George M. Green, MS "Recollections of Life in Mexico, 1853 to 1855"
  Charles James Papers
  Enrique Antonio Mejía Papers
  Matías Romero Correspondence (AHMR microfilm)
  Gaspar Sánchez Ochoa, original Mexican bond of 1865
  Plácido Vega Papers
California Historical Society, San Francisco, California
  George M. Green, photograph
  Plácido Vega, photograph
Indiana Historical Society, Indianapolis, Indiana
  Lew Wallace Collection
  José María Carvajal, photograph
  Lew Wallace, photograph
Indiana State Library, Indianapolis, Indiana
  Herman Sturm, photograph
Keith Ponsford Collection, 900 Creed Road, Oakland, California
  Augustín Alviso Papers
William Henry Seward House, Auburn, New York
  Matías Romero, photograph
Sonoma State Historical Park, Sonoma, California
  Mariano G. Vallejo Papers
United States National Archives, Washington, D. C.
  Dept. of State, Diplomatic Dispatches, Spain (Microcopy M-31, Roll 42)
  Dept. of State, Consular Dispatches, Ciudad Juárez (Microcopy M-184, Roll 1)
  U.S.–Mexican Claims Commission of 1868-76, Dockets 73–1015

II. GOVERNMENT DOCUMENTS

México. Legación. United States. 1866. *Correspondencia entre la legación de la república mexicana . . . con relación á la exportación de armas y municiones de guerra* [New York].
—— 1867. *Comisionados de la república mexicana en los Estados Unidos; dos notas de Señor Romero á Mr. Seward* [Baltimore].
—— 1867. *Responsabilidades contraídas por el gobierno nacional de México con los Estados-Unidos en virtud de los contratos celebrados por sus agentes, 1864–1867* [México].
—— 1868. *Circulares y otras publicaciones hechas por la legación mexicana en Washington durante la guerra de intervención, 1862–1867* [2 v., México].

—— 1868. *Contratos hechos en los Estados-Unidos por los comisionados del gobierno de México durante los años de 1865 y 1866* [México].
—— 1869. *Correspondencia de la legación mexicana en los Estados Unidos de América sobre los contratos celebrados por Don Juan Bustamante, 1862–1863* [México].
—— 1869. *Correspondencia oficial de la legación mexicana en Washington con el ministerio de relaciones exteriores de la república y el departmento de estado de Washington, sobre la conducta de D. Jesús G. Ortega, 1865–1866* [México].
—— 1870–1892. *Correspondencia de la legación mexicana en Washington durante la intervención extranjera, 1860–1868* [10 v., México].
México. Secretaría de Relaciones Exteriores. 1923–1938. *Archivo histórico diplomático mexicano* [40 v., México], **10, 12, 25, 30,** and Series 2, v. **1**.
—— 1899. "Necrologia de Matías Romero," *Boletín oficial* **7,** 1: pp. 169–171.
United States. Congress. *Congressional Globe.* 38th Cong., 1st Sess.
United States. Congress. House. *House Executive Document 100.* 37th Cong., 2d Sess.
—— *House Executive Document 1.* 38th Cong., 2d Sess.
—— *House Executive Document 20.* 39th Cong., 1st Sess.
—— *House Executive Document 73.* 39th Cong., 1st Sess.
—— *House Executive Document 1.* I, pt. 1. 39th Cong., 2d Sess.
—— *House Executive Document 33.* 40th Cong., 1st Sess.
United States. Congress. Senate. *Claims on the Part of Citizens of the United States and Mexico (Senate Executive Document 31).* 44th Cong., 2d Sess.
United States. War Department. 1880–1901. *The War of the Rebellion: A Compilation of the Official Records of the Union and Confederate Armies* [128 v., Washington].
—— 1896. *Index of Publications, Articles, and Maps Relating to Mexico in the War Department Library* [Washington].

III. NEWSPAPERS CITED

Denver, Colorado, *Post*
México, D.F., *Daily Mexican and Mining Press*
New Lork, New York, *Herald*
New York, New York, *Times*
Sacramento, California, *Daily Union*
San Francisco, California, *Alta California*
San Francisco, California, *Daily Morning Call*
San Francisco, California, *Daily Times*
Washington, D. C., *Chronicle*
Washington, D. C., *Star*

IV. OTHER SOURCES

ABBOT, GORHAM D. 1869. *Mexico and the United States; Their Mutual Relations and Common Interests* (New York).
ARIAS, JUAN DE DIOS. 1867. *Reseña histórica de la formación y operaciones del cuerpo de ejército del norte durante la intervención francesa* (México).
BADEAU, ADAM. 1888. *Grant in Peace; From Appomattox to Mount McGregor, A Personal Memoir* (Philadelphia).
BANCROFT, HUBERT HOWE. 1888. *History of Mexico* (6 v., San Francisco) **6**.
BARBER, AMHERST W. (ed.). 1914. *The Benevolent Raid of General Lew Wallace* (Washington).
BENJAMIN, RUTH. 1931. "Marcus Otterbourg, United States Minister to Mexico in 1867." *Publications Amer. Jewish Hist. Soc.* **32**: pp. 65–98.
BLUMBERG, ARNOLD. 1971. "The Diplomacy of the Mexican Empire, 1863–1867." *Trans. Amer. Philos. Soc.* **61, 8**: pp. 3–152.
BROWN, ROBERT BENAWAY. 1951. "Guns Over the Border: American Aid to the Juárez Government During the French Intervention." (Unpub. Ph.D. diss., Univ. of Mich.)
BUELNA, EUSTAQUIO. 1884. *Breves apuntes para la historia de la guerra de intervención en Sinaloa* (Mazatlán).
—— 1924. *Apuntes para la historia de Sinaloa, 1821–1882* (México).
BULNES, FRANCISCO. 1904. *El verdadero Juárez y la verdad sobre la intervención y el imperio* (México).
CADENHEAD, IVIE E., JR. 1972. *Jesús González Ortega and Mexican National Politics* (Fort Worth).
CALLAHAN, JAMES MORTON. 1909. "Evolution of Seward's Mexican Policy." *West Virginia Univ. Studies in Amer. Hist.* **1**: pp. 4–6.
—— 1932. *American Foreign Policy in Mexican Relations* (New York).
CALLCOTT, WILFRIED HARDY. 1965. *Liberalism in Mexico, 1857–1929* (Hamden, Conn.).
CHURCH, GEORGE EARL. 1866. *Mexico, Its Revolutions* (New York).
—— 1912. *Aborigines of South America* (London).
CORNWALL, W. A. 1871. "Maximilian and the American Legion." *Overland Monthly Mag.* **7**: pp. 445–448.
CORTI, EGON CAESAR [Count]. 1928. *Maximilian and Charlotte of Mexico.* Trans. by Catherine Alison Phillips (2 v., New York).
COSÍO VILLEGAS, DANIEL. 1955–1965. *Historia moderna de México* (7 v., México).
CRUZADO, MANUEL. 1905. *Bibliografía jurídica mexicana* (México).
DABBS, JACK AUTREY. 1963. *The French Army in Mexico, 1861–1867; A Study in Military Government* (The Hague).
Decrees of the Mexican Constitutional Republican Government Inviting American Emigrants to Settle in the Republic of Mexico. 1864. (New York and San Francisco.)
DOMENECH, EMMANUEL. 1868. *Histoire du Mexique: Juarez et Maximilian* (3 v., Paris).
DOMENECH, J. PASSAMA. 1866. *L'Empire mexicain, la paix, et les intérêts du monde* (México).
DUNIWAY, CLYDE AUGUSTUS. 1903. "Reasons for the Withdrawal of the French from Mexico." *Amer. Hist. Assoc. Annual Report, 1902* (Washington).
ESTRADA ROUSSEAU, MANUEL. 1952. "Postas de historia Sinaloense: casos y cosas de Don Plácido Vega." *Letras de Sinaloa* **5**: pp. 42–46.
—— 1954. "Postas de historia Sinaloense." *Letras de Sinaloa* **7**: pp. 21–25.
EVANS, ALBERT S. [Colonel]. 1870. *Our Sister Republic: A Gala Trip Through Tropical Mexico in 1869–70* (Hartford and San Francisco).
FITCH, FREDERICK G. 1870. *American and Mexican Joint Commission, Memorial of Frederick G. Fitch* (San Francisco).
FLINT, HENRY M. 1867. *Mexico under Maximilian* (Philadelphia).
FRAZER, ROBERT W. 1941. "Matías Romero and the French Intervention in Mexico." (Unpub. Ph.D. diss., Univ. of Calif., L.A.)
FRAZER, ROBERT W. 1942. "The Ochoa Bond Negotiations of 1865–1867." *Pac. Hist. Rev.* **11**: pp. 397–414.
—— 1944. "Maximilian's Propaganda Activities in the United States, 1865–1866." *Hisp. Amer. Hist. Rev.* **24**: pp. 4–29.
—— 1944. "The United States, European, and West Virginia Land and Mining Company." *Pac. Hist. Rev.* **13**: pp. 28–40.
—— 1946. "Trade Between California and the Belligerent Powers during the French Intervention in Mexico." *Pac. Hist. Rev.* **35**: pp. 391–399.
—— 1948. "Latin American Projects to Aid Mexico During the French Intervention," *Hisp. Amer. Hist. Rev.* **28**: pp. 377–388.
FRIAS Y SOTO, HILARIÓN. 1905. *Juárez glorificado y la intervención y el imperio ante la verdad histórica* (México).
FUENTES MARES, JOSÉ. 1962. *Juárez y la intervención* (México).
—— 1964. *Juárez y los Estados Unidos* (México).

GARCÍA, GENARO. 1904. *Juárez: refutación a Don Francisco Bulnes* (México).
GARCÍA, GENARO, and CARLOS PEREYRA (eds.). 1903–1911. *Documentos inéditos o múy raros para la historia de México* (36 v., Mexico) **1, 4, 13, 14**.
GODOY, JOSÉ F. 1898. *Enciclopedia biográfica de contemporáneos* (Washington).
GOLDWERT, MARVIN. 1965. "Matías Romero and Congressional Opposition to Seward's Policy Toward the French Intervention in Mexico." *The Americas* **22**: pp. 22–40.
GOODWIN, CARDINAL. 1930. *John Charles Frémont; An Explanation of his Career* (Stanford).
GONZÁLEZ ORTEGA, JOSÉ. 1941. *El golpe de estado de Juárez* (México).
GREEN, ALFRED A. 1870. *American and Mexican Joint Commission; Alfred A. Green vs. Mexico* (n.p.).
—— 1886. *A Vindication of Liberal Mexico, Being a Semi-Official History of the French Intervention* (New York).
GUZMÁN Y RAS GUZMÁN, JESÚS. 1930–1931. "Bibliografía de la reforma, la intervención y el imperio." *Monografías bibliográfias mexicanas* **17 & 19**.
HAMERSLY, THOMAS (ed.). 1881. *Complete Regular Army Register* (Washington).
HANNA, ALFRED JACKSON, and KATHRYN ABBEY HANNA. 1971. *Napoleon III and Mexico; American Triumph over Monarchy* (Chapel Hill).
HARRINGTON, FRED HARVEY. 1948. *Fighting Politician, Major General N. P. Banks* (Philadelphia).
HILDNER, ERNEST G., JR. 1950. "The Mexican Envoy Visits Lincoln." *Abraham Lincoln Qtly.* **6**: pp. 184–189.
HOBBS, JAMES [Captain]. 1875. *Wild Life in the Far West; Personal Adventures of a Border Mountain Man* (Hartford).
IGLESIAS, JOSÉ MARÍA. 1868. *Revistas históricas sobre la intervención francesca en México* (3 v., México).
IGLESIAS CALDERÓN, FERNANDO. 1905. *El egoísmo Norte-Americano durante la intervención francesa* (México).
—— 1907. *Rectificaciones históricas; las supuestas traiciones de Juárez* (México).
JOHNSON, ALLEN, and DUMAS MALONE (eds.). 1928–1936. *Dictionary of American Biography* (20 v., New York) **2**, "Francis Preston Blair."
KÉRATRY, EMILE [Comte de]. 1868. *La Contre-Guérilla française au Mexique* (Paris).
KNAPP, FRANK AVERILL. 1951. *The Life of Sebastián Lerdo de Tejada, 1823–1889* (Austin).
LALLY, FRANK EDWARD. 1931. "French Opposition to the Mexican Policy of the Second Empire." *Johns Hopkins Univ. Studies in Hist. and Pol. Sci.* **49**: p. 3.
LEFÈVRE, EUGÉNE. 1862. *Le Mexique et l'intervention européenne* (México).
LEOPOLD, RICHARD. 1940. *Robert Dale Owen: A Biography* (Cambridge, Mass.).
LOIZILLON, PIERRE HENRI. 1890. *Lettres sur l'expédition du Mexique, publiées par sa soeur, 1862–1867* (Paris).
MALLOY, GEORGE WALLACE. 1937. "The United States and the French Intervention in Mexico, 1861–1867." (Unpub. Ph.D. diss. Univ. of Calif., Berkeley.)
MARTIN, PERCY FALCKE. 1914. *Maximilian in Mexico; The Story of the French Intervention, 1861–1867* (New York).
MCCORNACK, RICHARD BLAINE. 1957. "Juárez y la armada norteamericana." *Historia Mexicana* **6**: pp. 493–509.
MCKEE, IRVING. 1947. *"Ben-Hur" Wallace: The Life of General Lew Wallace* (Berkeley).
MILLER, ROBERT RYAL. 1958. "Californians Against the Emperor." *Calif. Hist. Soc. Qtly.* **37**: pp. 192–214.
—— 1961. "The American Legion of Honor in Mexico." *Pac. Hist. Rev.* **30**: pp. 229–241.
—— 1961. "Gaspar Sánchez Ochoa: A Mexican Secret Agent in the United States," *The Historian* **23**: pp. 316–329.
—— 1962. "Herman Sturm: Hoosier Secret Agent for Mexico." *Indiana Mag. of Hist.* **43**: pp. 1–15.
—— 1962. "Plácido Vega: A Mexican Secret Agent in the United States." *The Americas* **19**: pp. 137–148.
—— 1963. "Lew Wallace and the French Intervention in Mexico." *Indiana Mag. of Hist.* **59**: pp. 31–50.
—— 1965. "Matías Romero: Mexican Minister to the United States During the Juárez-Maximilian Era." *Hisp. Amer. Hist. Rev.* **45**: pp. 228–245.
MONROY, GUADALUPE (ed.). 1965–1970. *Archivo histórico de Matías Romero; catálogo descriptivo, correspondencia recibida* (2 v., México).
MUSSER, JOHN. 1918. *The Establishment of Maximilian's Empire in Mexico* (Menasha, Wisconsin).
[NEW YORK. CITIZENS.] 1865. *Proceedings of a Meeting of Citizens of New York to Express Sympathy and Respect for the Mexican Republican Exiles, held at Cooper Institute, July 19, 1865* (New York).
—— 1866. *Dinner to Señor Matías Romero, Envoy Extraordinary and Minister Plenipotentiary from Mexico, on the 29th of March, 1864* (New York).
—— 1867. *Banquet to Señor Romero, Envoy Extraordinary and Minister Plenipotentiary from Mexico to the United States by the Citizens of New York* [Oct. 2] (New York).
NICOLAY, JOHN G., and JOHN HAY. 1890. *Abraham Lincoln, A History* (10 v., New York) **10**.
NIOX, GUSTAVE LEÓN. 1874. *Expédition du Mexique, 1861–1867; récit politique & militaire* (Paris).
NOLAN, JEANNETTE COVERT. 1943. *Hoosier City; The Story of Indianapolis* (New York).
OCAMPO, MELCHOR. 1900–1901. *Obras completas de Melchor Ocampo* (ed., Angel Pola, 3 v., México).
O'CONNOR, RICHARD. 1953. *Sheridan the Inevitable* (Indianapolis).
[OWEN, ROBERT DALE. 1866.] *Mexico. No. 1. Shall Our Government Act or Refrain from Acting in Mexican Affairs?* [n.p.].
—— *Mexico. No. 2. Historical and Financial Items.*
—— *Mexico. No. 3. Biographical Sketch of the Constitutional President of the Republic of Mexico; Juárez: Who and What is he?*
—— *Mexico. No. 4. Oppressions and Cruelties Resulting from French Intervention in Mexico.*
—— *Mexico. No. 5. General González Ortega and his Nine Endorsers Versus the Mexican Republic and the Constitutional President of its Unanimous Choice* (Washington).
—— *Mexico. What Shall Our Policy be?*
OWSLEY, FRANK LAWRENCE. 1959. *King Cotton Diplomacy: Foreign Relations of the Confederate States of America* (2nd ed., Chicago).
PAZ, IRENEO (ed.). 1888. *Los hombres prominentes de México* (México).
PERAL, MIGUEL ANGEL (ed.). 1944. *Diccionario biográfico mexicano* (México).
PÉREZ, JUAN E. (ed.). 1871. *Almanaque estadístico de las oficinas y guía de forasteros para el año de 1871* (México).
PERKINS, DEXTER. 1933. *The Monroe Doctrine, 1826–1867* (Baltimore).
FLETCHER, DAVID M. 1958. *Rails, Mines, and Progress: Seven American Promoters in Mexico, 1867–1911* (Ithaca).
PUIG CASAURANC, JOSÉ M. 1928. *Juárez, una interpretación humana* (México).
RAMÍREZ, ALFONSO FRANCISCO. 1948. *Hombres notables y monumentos coloniales de Oaxaca* (México).
RIPPY, JAMES FRED. 1926. *The United States and Mexico* (New York).
ROEDER, RALPH. 1947. *Juárez and his Mexico* (2 v., New York).
ROMERO, MATÍAS. 1867. *Biografía del ciudadano Benito Juárez* (Puebla).

—— 1892. *Artículos sobre México publicados en los Estados Unidos de América en 1891–1892* (México).
—— 1898. *Mexico and the United States* (New York).
—— 1960. *Diario personal de Matías Romero, 1855–1865* (ed., Emma Cosío Villegas, México).
SÁNCHEZ LAMEGO, MIGUEL A. 1952. *Generales de ingenieros del ejército mexicano, 1821–1914* (México).
SALM-SALM, FELIX C. [Prince]. 1868. *My Diary in Mexico in 1867 Including the Last Days of the Emperor Maximilian* (2 v., London).
SCHOFIELD, JOHN M. 1897. *Forty-six Years in the Army* (New York).
—— 1897. "The Withdrawal of the French from Mexico: A Chapter of Secret History." *Century Mag.* **54**: pp. 128–137.
SCHOLES, WALTER V. 1957. *Mexican Politics During the Juárez Regime, 1855–1872* (Columbia).
SCHROEDER, SEATON. 1887. *The Fall of Maximilian's Empire as Seen from a United States Gun-boat* (New York).
SCHURZ, CARL. 1911. *The Reminiscences of Carl Schurz* (New York).
SHERIDAN, PHILIP HENRY. 1902. *Personal Memoirs of P. H. Sheridan* (2 v., New York).
SMART, CHARLES ALLEN. 1963. *Viva Juárez! A Biography* (Philadelphia).
SOBIESKI, JOHN. 1907. *The Life Story and Personal Reminiscences of Col. John Sobieski* (Los Angeles).
—— 1919. *Life of President Benito Pablo Juárez* (St. Joseph, Mo.).
STURM, HERMAN. 1872. *American and Mexican Commission; Herman Sturm versus the Republic of Mexico* (Indianapolis).
STURM, HERMAN. 1869. *The Republic of Mexico and its American Creditors* (Indianapolis).
TURLINGTON, EDGAR W. 1930. *Mexico and Her Foreign Creditors* (New York).
TYRNER-TYNAUER, A. R. 1962. *Lincoln and the Emperors* (New York).
VAN DEUSEN, GLYNDON G. 1967. *William Henry Seward* (New York).
VEGA, PLÁCIDO. 1867. *Da cuenta al gobierno de la república mejicana sobre la comisión que le fué conferida al exterior* (Tepic, México).
[WALLACE, LEWIS]. 1906. *Lew Wallace: An Autobiography* (2 v., New York).
WELLES, GIDEON. 1911. *Diary of Gideon Welles, Secretary of the Navy Under Lincoln and Johnson* (3 v., Boston) 2.
WILGUS, A. CURTIS. 1932. "Official Expressions of Manifest Destiny Sentiments Concerning Hispanic America, 1848–1871." *Louisiana Hist.* **16**: pp. 486–506.
WOODMAN, LYMAN L. 1950. *Cortina: Rogue of the Rio Grande* (San Antonio).
WRISTON, HENRY M. 1929. *Executive Agents in American Foreign Relations* (Baltimore).
ZAMACOIS, NICETO DE. 1877–1882. *Historia de Méjico desde sus tiempos remotos hasta nuestros días* (18 v., México).

INDEX

Acapulco, 17, 30
Aguirre de la Barrera, José María, 18
Ainsa, J. M., 22
Allen, Lucretia, 9
Allen, William H., 34, 60
Almonte, Juan Nepumoceno, 5
Alviso, Agustín, 22
American Legion of Honor, organization of, 37–38, 60; commissioned by Juárez, 37–39; journey to Mexico, 38; in Mexico, 39–41; in Mexico City, 40–41; return to U.S., 41; subsequent claims, 41
Aranda, Silvestre, 39
Arellano, Felipe de, 18, 28
Argos, Juan, 27, 29
Arizona Exploring Expedition, 26–29
Arizona Territory, 25, 38
Armstrong, James, 24
Aros, Dolores, 22
Aspinwall, William H., 10
Austria, volunteer soldiers in Mexico, 7
Avalos, Crecencio, 25
Avery, Louis, 46, 52

Badeau, Adam, 16
Bagdad, 42, 44, 45, 60
Baja California, 12, 29, 31
Baltimore, 13, 34
Bancroft, George, 10
Banks, Nathaniel P., 59
Baranda, Pedro de, 56
Barraza, Pedro G., 18
Baz, Juan José, 56
Bazaine, François Achille, 7–8, 60
Beale, Edward F., 18–19
Beekman, James W., 10
Belgium, volunteer soldiers in Mexico, 7
Benítez, Justo, 56
Berriozábal, Felipe B., 58
Blair, Francis P., 14
Blair, Montgomery, 10, 14
Blanco Villaseñor, Sarmiento, 22
Blasdell, George, 40
Bolívar, Simón, 11
Brannan, Samuel, 31–33, 38
Brontes (ship), 23, 27–29, 31
Brown, Thomas, 19
Brownlow, James P., 44
Bruce, W. W., 28–29
Bryant, A. J., 24
Bryant, William Cullen, 10, 16
Buentello, Elizando, José, 25
Burke, Edmund, 19–20, 27–28
Burns, William, 29

California, 7, 13, 16–18, 20, 23, 25, 33, 38
Campbell, Judge, 28
Canada, 11, 14
Canales, Servando, 46, 52
Carlotta, Empress of Mexico, 7
Carmen Island, 18
Carvajal, José María, issues bonds, 30, 32–33, 44, 47, 60; meets Wallace, 42–43, 49; authority to recruit, 43, 48; commissioned to go to U.S., 43, 48–49, 60; exiled in Texas, 46–47, 52, 56; on Rio Grande, 46, 51–52, 56; returns to Mexico, 46, 51; early life of, 47–48; contract with Woodhouse, 49–50; railroad concessions, 49–50; death of, 52; as propagandist, 55
Cassill, F. M., 25
Castro, Victor, 22
Catalán, Francisco, 24
Cazotte, Charles de, 19–20, 27–28
Cervantes, A. L., 25
Charleston, 16
Chenery, Richard, 31–32
Chihuahua, 7–8, 12–13, 18, 29, 39, 48
Chile, 11–12
Chilpancingo, 17
Church, George Earl, 39, 46
Cincinnati, 13
Clark, James E., 29
Coahuila, 47
Coburn, John, 44
Colima, 8
Colombia, 11–12
Colon (ship), 28
Comonfort, Ignacio, 17
Confederate States of America, 8–11, 14, 24, 42–43
Cooke, Jay, 55
Corona, Ramón, 40, 60
Cortina, Juan N., 48
Corwin, Thomas, 12
Crabb, H. A., 24
Crawford, H. Clay, 44–45, 60
Cuba, 13

Davis, Edmundo, 45
Davis, Henry Winter, 10
Davis, Jefferson, 14, 23
Degallado, Santos, 48
Derbec, Etienne, 20
Días, Juan, 25
Díaz, Porfirio, 8, 17, 30, 40, 47, 56, 60
Dodge, William E., Jr., 16
Dominican Republic, 5
Dupin, Charles, 48
Durango, 7, 18, 36, 39, 47

Escobedo, Mariano, 30, 40, 45–47, 52, 60
Everman (ship), 46–47, 55–56, 60
Ewald, John, 29

Fellows, Thomas, 25
Field, Cyrus W., 46
Fitch, Frederick G., 31–33, 36
Flynn, H. C., 25
Ford, John S., 43–44
Forey, Louis Elie, 5–6
Foster, Robert S., 44
France, withdrawal of army from Mexico, 5, 7, 15; Counter-guerrilla unit, 6–7; navy in Mexico, 11, 18, 20
Frémont, John C., 10, 12, 33–36
Fuente, Juan Antonio de la, 18, 25–26
Fuentes y Muñoz, Jesús, 51
Fuerte, 17

García, Alejandro, 56
Geary, John W., 44
General McCallum (ship), 57
George, S. G., 24
Godoy, José A., 21
González Ortega, Jesús, prisoner of war, 30; exile in New York, 33; his supporters, 33–34, 52, 60; presidential claim, 33–34; relations with Wm. Allen, 34–35; returns to Mexico, 35–36
Grant, Ulysses Simpson, 9–11, 14–15, 42–43, 59
Great Britain, 5–6
Green, Alfred A., 31–32, 36, 38
Green, Francis L., 31, 38
Green, George Mason, early life of, 38; commands American Legion of Honor, 38–41; accepts surrender of Maximilian, 40; in Mexico City, 40–41; later life and death of, 41
Grinnell, Moses H., 50
Guadalajara, 30
Guatemala, 12
Guaymas, 33–35, 60
Guerrero, 8

Haines, Arthur, 39
Hahn, Albert, 29
Hammersley, John W., 10
Harris, C. W., 24
Haze (ship), 19
Henderson, William, 59
Herrera, Jesús, 25
Hoadley, David, 10, 46
Holliday, Benjamin, 16
Hubbard, Lorenzo, 25
Hungerford, Daniel E., 24, 28–29

Isabella II, Queen of Spain, 5

James, Charles, 19–20, 27
Jewett, D. John, 13
Johnson, Andrew, 14–15, 22, 26–27, 44, 55
Josephine (ship), 29
Juárez, Benito Pablo, opposes French, 5; suspends debt payment, 6; in San Luis Potosí, 6–7; in Chihuahua, 7–8, 39, 46, 48; in Durango, 7, 47; in Monterrey, 7, 46, 48; in Saltillo, 7; recognition by U.S., 7, 16, 23; in Mexico City, 8, 17; biography of, 10; and business concessions, 12; in Paso del Norte, 32, 38, 53; versus González Ortega, 33–34; and U.S. volunteers, 38–40; in Zacatecas, 39, 47
Juárez, Margarita Maza y Parada de, 12

Keoka (ship), 23, 29
King, Preston, 14

Labastida y Dávalos, Pelagio A., 5
Lake, Harvey, 38–39
La Reforma (War of the Reform), 5, 8, 17, 30, 48
Lee, Robert E., 14, 43
Leese, Jacob, 13
Lerdo de Tejada, Miguel, 17

INDEX

Lerdo de Tejada, Sebastián, 18
Lever, Edward A., 23, 29
Lewis, W. H., 27
Lincoln, Abraham, 7, 9–10, 14, 20, 22–23, 27, 42–43
Lincoln, Robert Todd, 9
Llorente, Manuel, 48
López, Gregorio, 25
Louisiana, 10
Low, Frederick, 22
Lozada, Manuel, 30

McClellan, George B., 10
McDougall, James, 10
McDowell, Irving, 20, 24
McNulty, George William, 39
Mancillas, Antonio, 24
Mancillas, Pedro, 20
Mare Island, 20, 25
Mariscal, Ignacio, 8
Matamoros, 7–8, 36, 39, 42, 46, 50–52, 56
Maximilian I, defeat of, 5, 8, 14, 16, 30, 40; establishment of empire, 6; recognition by U.S., 7, 10, 23, 55; execution of, 16, 37, 40; opposes French advisers, 60
Mazatlán, 17–18, 20, 30–32, 36, 50, 60
Maze, Montgomery, 25
Mazón, Donaciano, 26
Mejía, Enrique, 45
Mejía, Tomás, 44–45, 51–52
Mexican bonds, 8, 12, 18, 30, 32–33, 38, 44, 46, 49–52, 54–55, 58
Mexican clubs, 12–13, 17, 21–22, 25–26, 31–32, 38
Mexican empire, establishment of, 5; recognition of, 10, 23, 55
Mexican loans, 15, 27, 31–32, 43, 45, 48–49, 54–55
Mexico City, 6, 8, 16–17, 23, 30, 36, 38, 40–41, 57
Miller, Charles J., 25
Miramón, Miguel, 5
Miranda Viña, Joaquín, 25
Monroe Doctrine, 5, 10, 13–14, 17, 21, 23, 31, 34, 37–38, 42, 47, 55, 59
Monsuy, Anita, 30
Monterrey, 7, 46
Morelia, 7
Morgan, Edwin D., 50
Morillo, Precipiano, 25
Morton, Oliver P., 53
Mosby, John S., 44
Mosquera, Tomás de, 11

Napoleon III, 5–10, 15, 42
Navarro, Juan N., 12, 54
Netherlands (Holland), 12
Nevada Territory, 17, 24, 26
New Mexico Territory, 7, 38, 40
New Orleans, 8, 12–13, 36, 39, 40, 42, 44, 46, 51
New York, 7, 9, 11–13, 18, 32, 34, 36, 39, 41, 46–47, 49–51
Nord, Louis de la, 29
North Carolina, 15
Nuevo Leon, 30
Nuñez, Cuaristo, 25

Oaxaca, 7–8, 18
Ocampo, Melchor, 8
Ochoa, Juan José, 18
Orizaba, 6
Ortiz, Vicente, 27
Osborn, Albert H., 18
Osborne, Thomas O., 44, 46
Owen, Robert Dale, 55

Pacheco, Romualdo, 22, 26
Pacheco, Salvio, 22
Palacios, Adolfo, 29
Panama, 8
Paris, 15
Paso del Norte (Ciudad Juárez), 7, 32, 38
Patoní, José, 18
Pavón, Desiderio, 57
Peru, 11
Philadelphia, 15, 34
Plate, A. J., 27
Plumb, Edward Lee, 13
Plunkett, James B., 25
Pontiac (ship), 27
Puebla, 6, 17, 30, 56

Querétaro, 8, 30, 36, 38, 40, 57

Railroad concessions, 13, 33–35, 49–50
Ramonet, Francisco, 26
Reed, Arthur L., 44–45
Reform War. *See* La Reforma
Régules, Nicolás, 40, 60
Reynolds, Titus, 29
Rhin (ship), 20
Richmond, 14
Rio Grande, 7, 12–15, 23, 32, 37–38, 42, 44–46, 51–53
Robinson, Frederico, 25
Rock, A. D., 24
Rodríguez, Manuel, 21
Roland, Ernest C., 26
Romero, Matías, early life of, 8; in Washington, 8, 60; marriage of, 9; death of, 9; interviews U.S. presidents, 9, 44; banquets of, 10–11, 16; as propagandist, 10, 26; resigns, 12, 16; purchases arms, 13; and U.S. intervention, 14; contract with Schofield, 15; accomplishments of, 16; protests to U.S., 20; and Sánchez Ochoa, 32–33, 36; recruits U.S. volunteers, 44; and Carvajal, 49–50; coordinates secret agents, 54, 61
Roosevelt, Theodore, Sr., 16

Salm-Salm, Felix, 40
Saltillo, 7
Samuel F. Keese (ship), 58
San Diego (ship), 19
San Francisco, 12–13, 16–20, 22–28, 30–32, 38
San Luis Potosí, 6, 17, 30, 36, 48–50, 54
Sánchez Ochoa, Gaspar, early life of, 30; commissioned to go to U.S., 31; purchases arms, 31; recruits U.S. volunteers, 31, 35, 38; issues bonds, 32–33, 35, 60; as propagandist, 33; commission revoked, 33; gives rail concessions, 33; supports González Ortega, 34, 60; plans for military offensive, 35–36; asks for amnesty, 36; imprisoned in Mexico, 36, 60; death of, 36

Sanford, E. S., 46
Schofield, John M., 15, 44, 60
Schroeder, Seaton, 40
Segura, Eduardo, 25
Sepúlveda, Señor, 25
Serna, Jesús de la, 48
Seward, William H., relations with Mexico, 9–12, 44; and the Confederacy, 9, 14, 42; withdrawal of French from Mexico, 15, 59, 60; visits Mexico, 36, 41
Shearer, George B., 25
Sheldon, Lionel A., 44
Sheridan (gunboat), 56
Sheridan, Philip, 15, 39, 44, 51, 59
Sherman, William T., 14–15
Sinaloa, 12, 17, 20, 25, 29–31
Slaughter, James E., 43
Slidell, John, 9
Slosson, Edward, 31
Smith, Joseph (pseudonym of José Carvajal), 43
Sobieski, John, 40
Sonora, 7, 12, 31
Spain, 5–6, 11
Speed, James, 11
Spivalo, A. D., 22
Squier, Ephraim G., 37–38
Stanton, Edwin M., 44
Stocking, Wilbur F., 46–47, 52, 57
Sturm, Frederick C., 46, 56
Sturm, Herman, commissioned by Carvajal, 43–44, 49, 51–53, 59; sends ships to Mexico, 46, 55–58; negotiates bonds for arms, 51, 54–55, 60; early life of, 53; as propagandist, 55; compensation for services, 58–59; in Colorado and Mexico, 59; death of, 59
Sturm, Robert C., 54, 56–57
Sumner, Charles, 11
Suwanee (ship), 56

Tamaulipas, 42, 47–49, 52, 54, 56
Tampico, 47, 50, 57
Tapia, Santiago, 52
Tepic, 30
Texas, 7, 10, 14, 30, 33, 38, 41–44, 52
Thomas, John, 29
Tifft, Jonathan, 51
Togño, Juan, 34
Treviño, Andreas, 44
Tuttle, William H., 24
Tyler, Erastus B., 44

United States, Civil War, 5–11, 13–14, 16, 20, 23, 27, 34, 42–43, 49, 55, 60; volunteer soldiers in Mexico, 7–8, 12–15, 17, 23, 27, 30–31, 34, 37–41, 43, 52, 60
United States-Mexican Claims Commission, 36–37, 41, 47, 59
Urmy, John B., 29

Valdés, Jesús, 17
Vallejo, Mariano Guadalupe, 22
Vallejo, Uladislao, 22, 26, 29
Vanderbilt, Cornelius, 50
Vega, Plácido, in Calif., 16, 30; expenditures of, 16–17, 22; as propagandist, 17, 20–21, 26, 38; early life of, 17; financial resources of, 18, 27; commissioned to go to U.S., 18; purchases arms, 18–21;

supports Union party, 22–24; recruits U.S. volunteers, 23, 38, 60; in Chihuahua, 29, 39; a fugitive, 29–30; death of, 30
Vega, Sara, 30
Vega y Vega, Clara, 17
Vega y Vega, Plácido, 30
Velásquez, Romualdo, 25–26
Veracruz, 6, 8, 16, 48, 56–57
Veto (ship), 58
Victoire (ship), 20
Vigil, José María, 20–24
Villalón, Señor, 25
Villas, Eulalio, 48
Vixen (ship), 56

Walker, John G., 43
Wallace, Lew, founds Mexican Aid Society, 37, 44; confers with Juárez, 39, 46; early life of, 41; as Mexican general, 42–43, 49; his Texas peace plan, 42–43; meets Carvajal, 42–43, 49; on court-martial board, 43; orders Crawford to frontier, 44–45; recruits U.S. volunteers, 45–47, 51, 60; sails for Mexico, 46, 52, 55; in No. Mexico, 46–47; returns to U.S., 47; his compensation from Mexico, 47; and Mexican bonds, 49–51
Warner, Francisco, 24
Washington, D.C., 8–12, 14–16, 20, 23, 34, 37, 41, 43–44, 47, 49, 51, 60

Weitzel, Godfrey, 45
Williams, A.A.C., 26–29
Woodhouse, Daniel, 49–51
Woodhull, Maxwell Z., 44
Woodruff, W. E., 44
Wright, Horacio G., 59
Wulff, Erik, 13

Young, M. K., 39

Zacatecas, 36, 38–39, 47
Zaldo, Ramón de, 22, 24
Zaragoza, Ignacio, 6
Zihautenejo, 17
Zingarella (ship), 58